Writing
in the
21st Century

Past, Present, Future

A Carnegie Writers Publication

D1446015

The Carnegie Writers, Inc.
Educate.Write.Collaborate

Foreword
T.K. Thorne

Contributing Authors:
Carissa Barker-Stucky • Kristen Billingsley
Oluwakemi Elufiede • Tavia Garland
Kay Gragg • Bonnie Flynn
Jamie Hughes • LaDessa Mitchell
Tina Murray• Annie Laura Smith
Brian Smith • Jaden Terrel
Deborah Wilbrink

Editors
Carissa Barker-Stucky, M.F.A.
Oluwakemi Elufiede, M.Ed.

Contributing Editor:
Brian Smith

Cover Design
Carissa Barker-Stucky

•

Carnegie Writers, Inc.

Carnegie Writers, Inc. (CW) is a community-based 501(c)(3) non-profit organization for diverse writers and was inspired by The Carnegie Writers Group, founded in August of 2013 by Oluwakemi Elufiede.

The mission is to advance education, encourage collaboration, and provide resources for writing and literacy. The vision is to encourage children, adolescents and adults by providing positive and productive support in writing and literacy education based on personal goals.

Educate.Write.Collaborate

We Educate through workshops, tutorials, guest presentations, professional development training, and conferences.

We Write through power writing, progressive writing, and publications.

We Collaborate through group meetings, events, partnerships, and community-based programs.

CW conferences are held once a year in November and cover various topics in writing and literacy education. The purpose of the conference is to encourage professional and personal development.

This book was created in collaboration with the CW Conference Series, which is held once a year in November. It covers various topics in writing and literacy education. The purpose of the conference series is to encourage professional and personal development.

Table of Contents

Foreword   i
>   *T.K. Thorne*
Personal Growth and Development   1

Best Practices for   3
Productive Writing Groups
>   *Oluwakemi Elufiede and*
>   *Brian Smith*
Journal Writing: 11
The Key to Personal Growth
>   *Jamie Hughes*
Effective Written Communication   21
with Groups
>   *LaDessa Mitchell*

Marketing and Social Media   37

The Journey into Blogging   39
>   *Carol Roberts*
Writing Effective Book Reviews   51
>   *Annie Laura Smith*
Fiction Writing and the   61
World of Self-Publishing
>   *Kristen Billingsley*
Business Writing   75

Grant Writing :   77
Crafting a Sales Pitch Through Words
>   *Tavia Garland*
Writing Resumes and Cover Letters   95
for Success
>   *Bonnie Flynn*
Special Topics   109

Community Education: 111
Bridging the Gap to Creative Thinking
>   *Oluwakemi Elufiede and*
>   *Carissa Barker-Stucky*
Motivation and Writing   131
>   *Tina Murray*
Creating Characters with   145
Depth and Dimension
>   *Jaden Terell*
Constructing Better Fiction   165
>   *Kay Gragg*
Time to Tell: Writing Memoir   179
>   *Deborah Wilbrink*
Author Bios   197

Foreword
T.K. Thorne

Why did you open this book?

The answer has to do with something very basic about who you are—who *we* are.

We are the first words spoken around a fire. The first tale of hunting prowess or explanation of the inscrutable lightning, rainbows, the mystery of death. We are the recorders and shapers of history, the molders of culture, the spark and wind of ideas. We are the instructors, the teachers, the questioners, the interpreters, the keepers... And the twisters of knowledge. We are the archetypal Trickster, the shaman, the priest, the witch, the medicine man.

We are the storytellers.

We are novelist; historian; blogger; copy writer; memoirist; the writer of technical manuals, screenplays, lyrics or school books; the poet; the playwright. Storytelling is the origin and thread that runs through it all. The power of the word is illustrated by ancient wisdom: "The pen is mightier than the sword." So mighty, in fact, that, according to the Bible, the universe was created out of primordial chaos merely by the uttering a word. That is pretty powerful stuff.

I can assure you, I don't feel that powerful when I sit at my computer and decide multiple times I can't write a word until my coffee is exactly the right temperature or until I have won three games of solitaire in a row. Or, the idea of cleaning out my closet before starting to write becomes actually *tempting*.

Writing is hard work. That is, writing that works is hard work. Blaise Pascal, Benjamin Franklin, Henry David Thoreau, T.S. Elliot, and even Cicero have all apologized for long letters or stories, saying they did not have enough time to write a shorter one. We labor at our craft. We come to conferences. We read books on writing. We take something as enjoyable as reading a novel and stop to reread the most intense scene to figure out *why* there are tears running down our cheeks at the choice and arrangement of delicate little black letters on a white page.

If you do that, you are a writer. If you study people on a bus or strolling by in the mall, looking for idiosyncrasies for characters, or eavesdrop on conversations to sharpen your dialogue skills, or, if the sight of a knife on a table makes you wonder if you were a murderer how you would cover up the evidence, you are a writer.

If you get antsy separated from your computer or notebook and a closed door for too long, you are a writer. If you drive down the road with characters speaking to one another in your mind, or scenes unfolding, or words unraveling, and "wake up" to find you are somehow at your destination— or miles beyond it—, you are a writer. If you imagine what you would do if you were imprisoned in solitary confinement for years and the answer is write a book, even if it is in your head, you are a writer. If you imagine what it would be like to find out you have a fatal disease and what you would do with the time left, and the answer is finish your book, you are a writer. If you experience personal heartbreak or great joy and a little voice says, *Remember, this is how it feels*, so you can recreate it in words, you are a writer.

Writers are manipulators. That word in our culture has a sour taste, but it is true, and we need to embrace it. Don't you want your readers to laugh, cry, or say "aha!" in the right places? If you do not set it up right, keep them engaged, make them empathize, intrigue them, or evoke emotional reactions, you lose your reader, and that is the worst thing for a writer.

We may write first for ourselves, driven by the muse or the need to put bread on the table, but the reader is always there, even if we plan to stuff the manuscript in the drawer or burn it. We are storytellers. The first part of that is "story," and the second part is "tellers." They go together, and that is why you are listening to or reading these words. To be effective story-tellers, we must know our craft.

Learning to be a writer (which is, by the way, a perpetual state) is wonderful. We get to go where others or no one has gone before—a distant star, the depths of despair, back in time, or into the future. We explore the frightening, the unknown, our deepest dreams. We tell an old story with a new perspective. We can reinvent the world. Stephen King says, "Writing is magic, as much the water of life as any other creative art. The water is free. So drink."

Being a writer is powerful and wonderful, but it is also terribly confusing. We are told in order to be "good" writers, we must comply with confusing and odd rules: Write what you know. Show, don't tell. Start near the end. Kill your darlings. Avoid adverbs, passive tense, and "data dumps." Avoid prologues. Limit your descriptions. If it sounds like writing, rewrite it. Never use the word "suddenly." Apply dialect in dialogue sparingly. Write every day. Don't correct your first draft until you are finished. Then we are told that once we know the rules, we can break them. Some say we must break them. Confusing, indeed. Perhaps we need a new paradigm.

Which is a better color, cobalt or magenta?

The answer, of course, is totally subjective. So, too, is "good" writing. If you do not believe that, go read all the reviews of just about any book.

Stop trying to figure out the rules and whether your writing is "good." That is a surefire way to open the writer's Pandora box of self-doubt, self-criticism, and even depression. And, more importantly, it is the *wrong* question. It is not about whether your writing is "good;" it is about asking these three questions:

1. Does it work?
2. For whom?
3. How can it work better?

Changing the question from "Is it good?" to "Does it work?" redefines everything. Writing is not about rules; it is about tools. What are the tools I can use to make this work better for my historical fiction audience, my mystery audience, my scholar audience, or myself? When you ask these questions, your self-worth is not at stake. A criticism is a critique about whether the words are working, not a sword tearing your heart.

There are many tools to be found in this book. Use them to make your writing work better. And, no matter where you are on the journey—beginner or acclaimed author—I welcome you into the universal community of writers. Stories are our search— not for what is true, but for truths about our shared humanity. That is our task, our mission. It is who we are.

We are the storytellers.

Personal Growth
and Development

Best Practices for
Productive Writing Groups
Oluwakemi Elufiede and Brian Smith

Introduction
This chapter provides tools, techniques, and strategies that create, engage, and promote writing groups in various contexts. For example, resolutions include commitments, goals, and guidelines in a productive writing group for diverse writers. Solutions include writing group structure, exercises that support diverse learning styles, and writing genres. Furthermore, solutions create a writing community, writing accountability, and the writer-reader relationship. The resolutions and solutions lead to evolution and revolution. "Evolution" describes a writing group lifecycle: writing productivity with quantity, quality, and the identity of writers. "Revolution" relates to the impact of writing groups with professional and social support in the community. This chapter was inspired by Elufiede, Boden-McGill, & Cherrstrom (2015) presentation on productive writing groups.

The History of Writing Groups
According to Gere (1987), writing groups were established by institutions, intellectual traditions, and literary societies during the colonial period. These groups highlighted social dimensions and human interactions in formal and informal environments. They were grounded in collaborative learning, language development, and practical directions within literacy skills. Typically, formal environments that facilitate writing groups have a specific purpose of improving writing literacy and awareness of literary practice. Through these experiences, whether informal or formal, collaborative learning is prevalent because it includes

learner-centered approaches aimed at solving problems and having healthy debates. More importantly, language development improves vocabulary, dialectic, and socialization (Gere, 1987).

Best Practices

For effective implementation of best practices, the action plan must include four elements: create, engage, promote, and evaluate. Creation should fulfill a need in the community; engagement should be impacted by collaborative learning practices; promotion should be continuous and diverse; and evaluation should be open to constructive criticism and take steps towards active improvement. Reeves (2002) explains that real-time writing practices are based on collective energy.

Figure 1.1 The Action Plan

Create

Starting a writing group can present challenges. Some of the major questions are how many people will attend, how to advertise, and where the meetings will take place. First, determine the location, times, and days for meetings. The location should be an optimal environment for participants to get the most out of the writing group. Make sure the meeting place is comfortable and provides flexibility with meeting times and space. With any group, expect the unexpected as collaboration is the key to productivity within groups. Leadership is an important factor for specific leaders, co-leaders, or rotation. With leadership, members of the group should also be learning how to facilitate the group with innovative approaches. It is important to include group members in the decision-making process for setting the structure of the activities, feedback topics, goals, and rules. Without the inclusion of member ideas, there is no group. While the common interest in the group is writing, members have specific genres or writing interests. The group may need to develop subgroups that focus on specific topics of interest.

Engage

Engagement is integral to continuous participation and requires creativity. Members should actively participate in establishing mutual group guidelines that accommodate all members. Group meetings should include interaction activities such as free-writing, timed writing exercises, and word exercises. These activities encourage participation from all group members and also impact improvement of their individual writing skills. Free-writing is an activity that allows writers to express their past or current thoughts. Timed writing exercises may include writing prompts, collaborative writing, and word activities.

Along with the activities within in the group, members tend to develop personal relationships with group members outside of group meetings. Establishing relationships within the group can be initiated and encouraged through team-building activities that convey trustworthiness. This, in return, can lower participants' anxiety about sharing their writing projects. As members are working on individual projects, other members provide accountability for active productivity. Setting and managing goals can be difficult, so support offers reliability. There should be feedback based on the members' individual writing goals. For instance, if members share a specific project, they need to express to the group what type of feedback they are seeking so that it can be beneficial to their progress. For writers, sharing their writing can sometimes be problematic, so it is crucial that goals are set before the next group meeting. There should be an equal chance for members to share, and group reflection should be encouraged.

Promote

Promotion is a crucial element to ensure that members are productive in their individual writing projects. Writers want to be held accountable for their projects, so sharing and celebrating writing successes within the group is important. This also means that members should be encouraged to write not only in the group but also at home, making it a priority. There should be the inclusion of diverse writing resources related to group member interest. There should not be an expectation that members will remain in the group forever, though some will. The idea is that members will attend to get a need met and, ultimately, feel more confident about writing. Additionally, there must be a healthy transition of new and old members that attend meetings consistently.

Advertisement for the group in various places will reach more interested members. Three major marketing techniques for membership are social media, community partners, and word of mouth. Since 1997, social media has impacted communication, relationships, employment, and the economy. Because of this, group leaders should discuss structure and recruitment as it relates to social media. The following question should be considered for promotion: does the group want a website, Facebook, Twitter, Instagram and/or Blog? Some social media networking can present challenges, so member suggestions will provide the group with the ability to make a sound consensus that will benefit the group's longevity. Based on the group meeting location, the community partners can help with promotion in newspapers, newsletters, online events, and/or news media. With a variety, word of mouth is guaranteed to influence membership.

Evaluate

Evaluating writing is one of the most beneficial practices of a writing group, but it can be difficult to execute effectively. One thing writing group members should be aware of is how much they are evaluating. Providing too much negative feedback can overwhelm and discourage a writer while providing too much positive feedback can leave a writer unchanged. Instead, the evaluator should pick two to three elements in most need of revision and focus on a detailed suggestion of *how* to change these elements. In addition, group members must understand the difference between criticism and critique. A "critique" is a detailed evaluation of something while "criticism" generally has a connotation of negative judgement. Writing groups should always strive for critique and give balanced evaluations.

The current stage of the writing defines what to evaluate. An early draft should not be read for mechanical errors such as grammar mistakes and syntax. These local problems should only be worked out when polishing a piece of writing. There is no use in correcting the grammar of a paragraph that is going to be taken out or revised. Instead, group members should focus on global issues, or changes that take the entire piece of writing into consideration. For example, if critiquing fiction, an evaluator could make the suggestion to add more sensory detail throughout a piece and name some specific places that need it the most.

Six elements to keep in mind while critiquing creative writing are voice, tone, style, diction, characters, and point of view. Elements like voice and style are unique to each writer, and tuning these qualities is one of the most important improvements a writer can make. A writer's voice is what distinguishes them from everyone else, and writing groups can help identify and change the quality of this voice. Elements like diction and tone inform this voice and are often a good place to start in critique. Other elements like characters and point of view are less connected to the voice of a writer and more to the craft of writing. Character and point of view are vehicles for a story to grow, and experimenting with these through writing groups can be extremely beneficial.

One strength unique to writing groups is that all evaluation is peer review. A traditional evaluation setting includes a teacher and a student. The teacher is seen to have the answers while the student is supposed to listen and learn. This dynamic can be limiting for a few reasons. First, writers only get one opinion on their writing. Second, it does not give the writer any options on what to change. Navigating through the comments of writing peers can take a little longer but is ultimately more rewarding. In a peer review setting, writers decide which comments to use for revisions and which comments to discard. Giving writers this choice makes the evaluation process more personal and effective.

Reflection
Successful writing groups require everyone to be engaged and able to participate equally. Factors like location, meeting time, group goals, and rules should accommodate everyone. Collaboration is important in writing groups; these factors can make or break the group. For example, if a group is focusing on a topic in which only half of them are interested, then it loses the creative energy of everyone uninterested.

Conclusion
Open communication for both the writing and the group itself is necessary for the group dynamic. Developing healthy relationships depends on all these factors because writers are part of a larger community. Being a part of this community includes access to conferences, retreats, residencies, continuing education courses, joining associations, and reading events. Groups must be promoted. With that, community is crucial between group members as writing groups need to be connected with the larger community around. This expansion enhances best practices for future writing groups.

References

Elufiede, K., Boden-McGill, C., & Cherrstrom, C. (2015). *[Re]solutions and [R]evolution: Adult Learning Practices for Productive Writing Groups.* Session presented at American Association for Adult and Continuing Education Conference, Oklahoma City, OK.

Gere, A. R. (1987). *Writing groups: History, theory, and implications.* Carbondale: Published for the Conference on College Composition and Communication Southern Illinois University Press.

Reeves, J. (2002). *Writing alone, writing together: A guide for writers and writing groups.* Novato, CA: New World Library.

Journal Writing:
The Key to Personal Growth
Jamie Hughes

Henry David Thoreau (1962) surmised:

> Is not the poet bound to write his own biography? Is there any other work for him but a good journal? We do not wish to know how his imaginary hero, but how he, the actual hero, lived from day to day.

Numerous journals and diaries published throughout the decades describe the personal thoughts and feelings of some of history's most famous, and even infamous, citizens. Through mere pages in a book, we can share the heartbreak of a crying mother who just lost her precious newborn to disease, the fear of a young girl and her family hiding behind a secret wall while armed soldiers search the house, and the gut-wrenching guilt of a US President after making a devastating war time decision. Equally as important, these published journals give readers a unique glimpse into history. They are present as the waves crash against the bow of the first boat to land at Jamestown, standing in the oval office as world-changing decisions are made, and sitting on the roof of an apartment building as a crowned rock star shoots up heroin while contemplating the emptiness of fame. Key figures such as Helen Keller, Ronald Reagan, Ralph Waldo Emerson, Captain John Smith, and Virginia Woolf kept personal journals. Many cherished writings were not from public figures. One of the most famous diaries published, *The Diary of a Young Girl* by Anne Frank, details the grim circumstances endured by a common family during World War II. The author shared daily musings about her hopes, dreams, fears, and normal teenage drama. The tone of her writings changed drastically, however, after her family was forced into hiding because of the Nazi occupation during the war. While many of us cannot imagine living through an experience like that, we readers have the privilege of seeing it, hearing it, and feeling it all because a normal, average young girl decided to keep a personal journal. The young Miss Frank (1967) reveals:

> Writing in a diary is a really strange experience for someone like me. Not only because I've never written anything before, but also because it seems to me that later on neither I nor anyone else will be interested in the musings of a thirteen-year old school girl. Oh well, it doesn't matter. I feel like writing.

Time and millions of readers have proven her wrong. Just as these now-historical figures gained great benefit from the process of personal writing, you can, too. Studies continue to show that people who write regularly in a journal experience better emotional, spiritual, and physical health. The proven methods and disciplines of personal writing allow anyone to take advantage of the growth and benefits. An added bonus for the aspiring author is the rich material gained from their intimate outpourings. The characterizations, settings, experiences, and emotions provide a taste of reality that engages readers, now and for years to come. The biggest payoff may even prove to be historical.

Personal Writing

Personal writing takes on many forms, one of which is journal writing. Is there a difference between a diary and a journal? Not necessarily in theory but certainly in practice. Historically, diary writing has carried the connotation of boring or trivial daily reports that seem more of a rote chore than an enjoyable experience. Even though classic examples of diaries have provided valuable information about the historic details of life during by-gone eras, many people are turned off by the idea of this style of writing.

The non-conforming styles of journal writing, however, more resemble having an intimate conversation with your best friend. Several writing methods are compatible with journaling, such as personal reflection, poetry, autobiographical, lists, fiction, letter writing, and others. Whether the author flourishes within the boundaries of structured exercises or prefers the liberty of free-writing, the wide variety of styles provides the perfect prescription for individual expression.

Writing in a journal has innumerable benefits, many of which are so powerful that some people notice a difference in mood after only a few entries. This incredible tool helps people to heal from trauma and past hurts in a way that often rivals treatment involving only therapy. Written from the privacy of one's own home, the journal is available night and day to record thoughts and feelings without judgement or fee. It allows the processing of difficult emotions at a pace that is both natural and comfortable. By dating each entry, another benefit of journaling is discovered. Documenting life allows for reflection, especially reviewing the progress of personal goals. Deeper reflection over time reveals patterns of circumstances throughout life and patterns of personal responses to those circumstances. Reviewing those allows you to strengthen your resolve or redirect your outlook on life. In other words, do you like where you are or do you need to make some changes in order to go a different direction in life? This review method is called "introspection," and it leads to growth. Personal growth comes from examining your current position, gaining a vision for where you would like to be, and then moving purposefully in that direction. Abraham Maslow quipped, "You will either step forward into growth or you will step backward into safety" (Tracy, 2010). Benjamin Franklin applied the same principle when he advised, "Without continual growth and progress, such words as improvement, achievement, and success have no meaning" (Connor, 2013).

Methods

All new skills have one thing in common— a starting point. Many people who are interested in the benefits of personal writing wonder about the best way to start writing in a journal. As the old adage goes, the journey of a thousand miles begins with one step. Beginning can seem like a daunting task, but there are several options to help the novice or returning writer get started. One of the easiest ways to learn is to take a class. Classes may be offered at the local library or community college, online or as part of a private group. Search online or make some calls to find one that will work for you. If you have to travel for a short time or pay for the class, then you should. It is worth it. The investment made will be of greater value than the expense. Another option is to purchase a book on the subject. For the aspiring author, continuous reading about the topic of writing should be part of ongoing learning and growth. There are far too many titles to list here, but, again, a little research will pay off. Try and find at least one that will expound upon the psychology behind personal writing, so you will have a greater understanding of how your emotions are tied to events in your life. That understanding will not only help you process events and relationships but also provide clear details for later use. There are many books and online sources, such as *Writing for Well-Being*, that offer writing prompts to lead writers through various topics or exercises, challenging them to use their creativity (Writingforwellbeing.net, 2014). These unique catalysts aid writers by asking deep, insightful questions or leading them into quirky and interesting story starters. The goal, either way, is to initiate the writing process or to stir the imagination. The way to develop any new skill is practice, practice, practice. Vladimir Horowitz, one of the greatest pianists of all time, affirmed, "The difference between ordinary and extraordinary is practice" (Flatau, 2015). To gain the benefits of personal writing, you must do it consistently.

Consistency

Consistency is the name of the game when it comes to healing, growth, and introspection as well as generating fantastic writing material. Consistency takes determination and planning. Determination comes from the "why" — the reason you are writing. For the sake of this discussion, the reason for writing in a journal is personal healing, growth, and emotional well-being. That perspective will bring out intimate, original material that can be harvested for professional writing. Poetry, short stories, novels, plays, songs— all of these are inspired by the heart of the writer in order to reach the heart of the reader. The audience wants to relate; they want to be touched, excited, emotionally connected; they want to be part of the story. This can only come from an authentic piece. Planning requires an effort to examine your time and goals. What do you want to accomplish? How much time do you have? Knowing yourself will allow you to realistically set goals for writing. If you work well with structure, then schedule daily blocks of time to write, even if it is only 30 minutes. If you work better with inspiration, keep a journal with you always so that you can write about interesting experiences as they happen. Whichever method works for you, do not give up. Keep going, even when you do not feel like it. It may be simple, but it will not always be easy.

Another way to remain consistent is to engage in writing prompts and writing classes or groups. Prompts, as stated before, give you an opportunity to write about something you would not normally consider. We, as humans, tend to stay within our own circle of thought. Be intentional about stretching yourself. Explore areas outside of your realm of comfort. Do not allow yourself to accept complacency. Find writing classes or groups in your area or online. These have more value than most people imagine. Even if you are currently published and already writing in some capacity, you can always learn something from an instructor or another writer. An investment in improving your skills is an investment in yourself. If there are no writing groups in your area, create one. The ability to reach out to others in your community with similar interests is right at your fingertips.

Professional Material

Nin (1947) recalled, "It was while writing a diary that I discovered how to capture the living moments. Keeping a diary all my life helped me to discover some basic elements essential to the vitality of writing." Generating source material from personal journal writing is like perusing family photo albums, looking for those special snapshots that evoke instant emotions. In essence, capturing pictures of real life and translating them to story form is the key, but it must be authentic. The raw vulnerability of the writer's day to day life provides an authenticity that easily connects with readers' feelings and experiences. Parts of the story, such as setting and characterization, become more relatable.

As stated earlier, one of the main benefits of keeping a journal is introspection. There is no greater way to get to know yourself— your fears, hopes, dreams, frustrations, and joys— than sharing your innermost thoughts and feelings on paper. This process allows the writer to garner insight into the true human experience, not just a two-dimensional facsimile to be used as a character in a book. Writing in this manner helps develop strong writing skills. Along with any other skill, whether it be artistic or athletic, practice is necessary to build effective writing technique and to develop a unique voice. Your authentic voice, the part of your spirit and heart that has something to say, can only emerge if you learn how to release it. You may have to dig through years of dirt to uncover it, but it is there, and the only way for that gem to sparkle is to keep polishing it. The longer you consistently write, the greater the range of experiences and emotions you will divulge. As you explore the changing times of your life, you will travel down the roads that are uniquely yours to discover. The lessons you learn about your own outlook on life, your beliefs about yourself and the world in which you live, are immeasurable. At the same time, those areas within yourself that are common to all mankind emerge, leading you to a destination that any reader can visit with familiarity. The trick, however, is to write for yourself, not for an audience. Cyril Connolly (1933) wisely remarked, "Better to write for yourself and have no public, than to write for the public and have no self."

Introspection is not the only means of journal writing that can produce greater understanding and fantastic material for professional writing. Careful observation of the surrounding world creates awareness of circumstances that affect everyone on a daily basis. Take time to reflect on your surroundings through writing highlights— the little details in settings and people throughout life that often go unnoticed. Carefully writing about the details of a surrounding environment builds dimension into the skills of aspiring authors. Take this story excerpt for example: the main character's daily commute to work involves seeing the same run-down furniture store on the corner of 5th and Wilkesboro that has the N burned out in their open sign so it reads OPE, which has created a nagging desire for her to stop in and ask if anyone named Opie works there. With just a little observation, the author can use a detail from real life to add dimension which not only reads well, but can also lead to a recurring theme, a funny character trait, or a unique setting for later interactions.

Another superb use of your personal writing is as a source for characters. Whether working on a novel, short story, play, or other masterpiece, using personality traits from people in real life will add depth and believability to fictional characters. Almost all fiction has an element of truth, and most famous writers base characters off of real people, even only a portion of that character resembles the original. Some fictional characterizations are an amalgamation of several actual people. This method should be used with caution, however. Writing about a real person without their permission could lead to legal action. Characters should fit the needs of the story with life-like traits written into them, not merely clones of the real person with a superficial name change (Writersrelief.com, 2009). Writing about Uncle Larry but changing his name to Gary will not work. Learning the skill of character development can be accomplished through personal writing by routinely spending time writing about people that you know or interact with on a regular basis. Detailing their quirks and peculiarities will provide rich material that can be integrated into later works or superimposed onto fictional characters.

Conclusion

The incredible benefits from personal writing can be gained only through experience, which comes only from consistency. Compare it to purchasing a gym membership: joining the gym will not get anyone in shape until they do the work. The same applies to journal writing— benefits are awarded only after putting in the necessary time and effort. Personal writing becomes richer and fuller over time. It not only serves as an outlet for deep thoughts and emotions and as an inlet for growth and understanding but also becomes much more: a natural part of the writer, a written embodiment of their spirit. Along with the immense personal benefits, professional material surfaces as a natural outcome. For all that writing is and all that it accomplishes, Victoria Field's (2006) poem *Why Writing?* provides the definitive answer to a universal question:

It says the unsayable.
Gives voice to the voiceless.
It's a lifetime's work -
Handiwork, whole body work.
It gives form to chaos.

Past, Present, Future

It reflects the present moment,
Changes the past
And creates the future.
It can exist forever
Or completely disappear.
It is what it is.
It can always be changed.
It's where the impossible
Becomes the possible.
It takes us out of ourselves
And into ourselves.
It is where we live our unlived lives,
Where we can surprise ourselves.
It is fire.
Only we can write our writing.

References

Bolton, G., Field, V., & Thompson, K. 2006. *Writing works: A resource handbook for therapeutic writing workshops and activities.* London: Jessica Kingsley.

Connolly, C. (1933). *New Statesman.*

Connor, J. (2013). Words to Motivate You. *Dr. Julie Connor.* Retrieved July 11, 2016, from http://www.drjulieconnor.com/words-to-motivate-you/

Flatau, T. (2015). *Raising your game through purposeful practice.* Retrieved July 11, 2016, from https://www.linkedin.com/pulse/raising-your-game-through-purposeful-practice-tom-flaau?forceNoSplash=true

Frank, A. (1967). *The Diary of a young girl.* Garden City, NY: Doubleday.

How to write fiction based on real life [Web log post.]. (2009). Retrieved July 10, 2016, from http://writersrelief.com/blog/2009/04/how-to-write-fiction-based-on-real-life/

Nin, A., & Burford, W. 1947. *On Writing.* Yonkers, NY: O. Baradinsky.

Thoreau, H. D., Torrey, B., & Allen, F. H. (1962). *Journal.* New York: Dover Publications.

Tracy, B. 2010. *How the best leaders lead: Proven secrets to getting the most out of yourself and others.* New York: American Management Association.

Writing for Well-Being. *Therapeutic Writing.* (2014). Retrieved July 10, 2016, from http://www.writingforwellbeing.net/

Effective Written Communication with Groups

LaDessa Mitchell

To be successful in any career, strong communication skills are paramount. In addition to strong interpersonal skills and team-oriented skills, communication skills are one of the top three criteria used by recruiters to evaluate job candidates for management positions (Kinnick and Parton, 2005). Job candidates are expected to communicate well in one-on-one situations and in group scenarios. Employers' expectations of graduating students' written communication skills include clarity of expression, correct language, and specificity of message (Attan et al, 2012). Therefore, it is imperative of faculty and staff in higher education to emphasize the importance of these skills to their students and provide them a toolkit of different means to express themselves effectively.

Preparing students and potential job candidates for the communication demands of their industry requires being current on the ever-evolving technology used to communicate. Advances in technology have allowed for more constant and personally engaging communication with more diverse groups of people. Learning experiences from working in groups help students create meaningful content in a variety of contexts and build the literacy needed to develop the proficiency required in today's workplace (Staggers, Garcia, & Nagelhout, 2008). The ability to collaborate without being bound by physical constraints and work across functional roles brings new opportunities and obstacles to communication in the workplace on an interpersonal and intrapersonal level. (Kudesia & Elfenbein, 2013). The transmission of important information has become more efficient, yet it does not come without an increased level of complexity. Increased exposure to different ways of employing written group communications is vital to navigating the complexity of using different technologies to send information while maximizing their efficiency.

Kudesia and Elfenbein (2013) believed, "leaders must be cognizant not only of their nonverbal behaviors, but also of the nonverbal behaviors of others and how the collective influence can affect culture, performance, and other outcomes" (p. 819). Factors that should be considered when deciding the type of group communication to be employed include the relationship between the receiver and sender, the sensitivity of the information being communicated, and the need for future accessibility to the conversation. The sociocultural factors that shape communication can create quite a challenge when competing interests and conflicting schedules are in play. This chapter will focus on this example to explore the many ways to communicate within the context of a group.

The Importance of Written Group Communication
Effective group communication is at the core of our society. From the founding documents guiding our federal government to the employee manuals governing our workplace, written group communication has been vital to the transmission of important information to large groups of people and the synergy with which that can function. Complexity in written communication is attributed to the increase in individuality and speed desired in communication. For instance, one-on-one forms of communication may be the preference for tough conversations, such as termination of employment or presentation of improvement plans, given the sensitivity of the information being communicated and the relevance of the conversation to future decisions. However, something as simple as scheduling a staff meeting can be done with less consideration. Written

communication can now be in digital form and disseminated simultaneously within seconds to multiple receivers. The instantaneous nature of written communication demands that individuals must develop new skills to be proficient in their writing, despite their proficiency in face-to-face-communication (Cardon & Marshall, 2015). In an era when emotional intelligence and relationship-building through verbal and nonverbal communication is a vital part of the workplace experience (Patterson, 2012), conveying a message that is concise yet considerate can be difficult. To understand how written group communication has shaped our workplaces, one needs to look at how it has functioned over time.

History of Workplace Communication

In the 1960s, the primary form of communication was a face-to-face meeting, with letters and telegrams as secondary methods when distance thwarted in-person meetings. Computers made their debut in the 1970s and 1980s; however, it was the fax machine that transmitted timely messages for a nominal cost (Media Platform, 2015). Mobile phones became available in the 1990s and broke the need for time boundedness or cost constraints to make a business phone call from the office. When email was introduced in the late 1990s, workplace communication changed forever. The 2010s brought about new technology that enhanced phone capabilities, video communication, and the ability to scan documents, which diminished the need for a fax machine. Zehr (1998) notes a major shift from an industrial economy to an information society, and an office economy caused a parallel shift in workplace values to integrity, communication, and flexibility.

Kinnick and Parton (2005) reviewed the role of communication and individual communication competencies of contestants from the first season of the television show *The Apprentice*. While the art of persuasion was critical to success in the weekly challenges, it was a contestant's leadership ability and interpersonal skills that were valued by teammates. Kinnick and Parton define "interpersonal skills" as the ability to work on teams, teach others, serve customers, lead, negotiate, and work well with people from culturally diverse backgrounds (p. 431).

Sharing and building upon experiences in a group setting is connected to the Real Life Approach to perfecting the use of language to convey a message in the workplace. However, most trainers and educators abide by the Component's Ability Approach (Canale and Swain, 1980). This approach considers mastery of communication in the workplace a product of the ability to perform specific tasks in an effective way. To be competent in communication, one must be competent in areas of sociolinguistics, linguistics, and strategic discourse (Attan et al., 2012). Robles (2012) discovered that "potential employers want to hire applicants with strong interpersonal skills, but new graduates are falling short of employers' expectations" (p. 459). Mastery of communication skills takes practice and experiential learning, which can be acquired through the necessary collaboration of group projects.

Goals of Written Group Communication
Moving from face-to-face team exercises to an online platform without adaptations for the change in environment can be difficult (Staggers, Garcia, & Nagelhout, 2008). Technology can enhance the way we communicate and help to overcome barriers beyond time, proximity, and culture (Cardon & Marshall, 2015). However, it does not have the ability to clarify a message because this requires the originator of the message to have an understanding of the context and the intended audience.

Diversity of Thought and Expertise
Along with the changes in tools used to communicate, the individuals with whom we communicate have changed over the past decades. There are more women in the workforce, and as the population of the US becomes more diverse in racial and ethnic

make-up, this fact is reflected in the workplace from the bottom to the top. People are living longer and remaining in the workforce longer, so the work environment has to accommodate multiple generations and age groups. While the older generations value loyalty to jobs and longevity with companies, young workers seek flexibility and want to achieve a positive work-life balance. This is evident in the communication style of each generational group. Generation X and Millennials/Generation Y/Generation Z seek out a variety of career interests and pursuits beyond the typical 40-hour work week, and this means that the average worker is multi-faceted in their expertise (Goudreau, 2015). For example, an entry-level accountant may work as a successful wedding photographer on the weekends. This means they mastered the skills of their day job but also possess transferable skills and specialized skills applicable to photography.

Advancements in Technology

The early 2000s brought about intranet, a virtual space for internal documents to live and for interoffice communication (Media Platform, 2015). The number of people using a particular type of technology for communication is driven by the wide adoption of the technology. Baharun and Suleiman (2008) indicate that the broader factors of globalization, internationalization, and competition are propelling these advancements and preferences for communication. The emergence of social networking platforms, such as Facebook and LinkedIn, have pushed email to second place in terms of the most popular form of interpersonal business communication; however, it has yet to dominate email communication in the workplace (Cardon & Marshall, 2015). Some social networking platforms (SNPs) are designed specifically for company use and customized based on the organization's needs. Proponents of SNPs value the interactive, bottom-up approach that requires self-organization and facilitates innovation while skeptics downplay the value, noting the software security issues, widespread adoption, the replacement or richer sources of communication, and the way this impacts the organizational structure (Cardon & Marshall, 2015).

Types of Communication

Traditional communication channels include email, face-to-face unscheduled conversations, face-to-face scheduled meetings, calls on landline phones, and calls on mobile phones while emerging communication tools such as document sharing, wikis, texting, instant messaging, private messages on social networks, and group messages on social networks make room for new channels to deliver messages (Cardon & Marshall, 2015). Of the many methods available to use, two formats convey information: verbal and written. The use of electronic means overlaps both of these categories, with opportunities to accommodate for nonverbal cues.

The best type of communication to use depends on the content of the message, the setting or environment, the audience, and the messenger. However, Cardon and Marshall (2015) discovered that in the modern evolving workplace, traditional forms of communication such as face-to-face conversations, both scheduled and unscheduled, and phone calls are the most preferred methods for communication in teams and one-on-one. This is likely because these methods result in effective teamwork that promotes innovation, higher productivity, and engagement among employees. Cardon & Marshall (2015) noted that virtual collaboration also drives productivity with faster "decision-making speed, decision quality, and team collaboration" (p. 278).

Spoken (or Verbal) Communication

In the workplace, verbal communication would take place by meeting with a person in their office or in a conference room. The telephone is also a suitable and standard form of communication. The presentation of shared values, beliefs, norms, thinking, and expectations are communicated in verbal and nonverbal communication throughout the workplace from the initial interview through the discontinuation of employment (Attan et al, 2012; Kudesia & Elfenbein, 2013). In groups, verbal communication can occur face-to-face with each individual physically present or through electronic means, with a hybrid or full virtual presence.

Groups who meet in-person have advantages in communication. The ability to both read nonverbal cues and pick up on social cues is a valuable facet of communication. Even the way a person is dressed can speak volumes. Many employers are seeking applicants who meet qualifications based on training and prior experience, yet the value of those attributes can be diminished by low emotional intelligence. Effective communication is paramount to success as it contributes to the way a message is communicated; more importantly, effective communication creates opportunities to present a message to a broad audience.

Although participants may not have a visual of those in communication, language and voice inflexions can provide clues to a topic of discussion. GIFs and memes have gained popularity because they add a missing dimension to verbal electronic communication that cannot be communicated adequately through modes such as text messages, voice messages, and phone calls. Conference calls are a popular form of communication that transcends the obstacle associated with distance and convenience.

Written Communication

Every message should have three parts: an introduction, the body of the message containing your main points, and a conclusion. Depending on the form of communication, additional components may be required (Thornbury & White, 2007). Before the establishment of email addresses, people used physical mailing addresses and mail stops to send important messages to their recipients. Typewritten letters on nice stationery with formal letterhead provided information about major decisions.

Memorandums, or memos, were used as a concise way to inform employees about new policies and changes to policies in place prior to the advent of email. These messages are a form of top-down communication that originates from management or supervisors to subordinates. It is a form of internal workplace communication.

As the workplace moves toward more efficient and timely ways to communicate important information, these archaic forms are not prevalent in the 21st century workplace. However, in a large workplace that has a workforce with a full spectrum of generations, seeing an official letter or memorandums drafted and disseminated as an attachment to an email is not unusual.

Many of the current methods of electronic communication are based on the format of the original letter and memorandum. Figure 2.1 below shows the components these forms of communication have in common and gives a glimpse of the technological evolution.

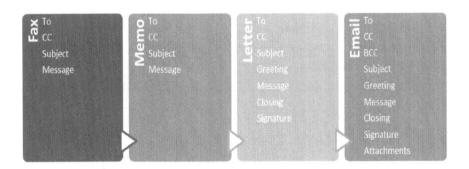

Figure 3.1 Components for Forms of Communication

Instant messenger software and the shift from pagers to mobile phones with text message capabilities helped deformalize communication yet improved speed and succinctness. Technology allowed people to send short messages quickly and to connect with multiple users at the same time. With social media and networking websites and software, the ability to connect is virtually limitless. While those who are engaged in one or more forms of these communication channels can receive written communication 24 hours a day, 7 days a week, they should not be contacted around the clock. Many individuals physiologically operate on the eight-hour work day, five-day work week and understand the disadvantages associated with staying too connected. It is important to exercise courtesy and respect when engaging in communication with others, especially in a group. Take the timing of the message and privacy of the recipient into consideration.

How to Communicate in Groups

Attan et al (2012) noted that "Written communication has a role in organizational processes" and has "important roles in performing or causing actions" (p. 77). The effectiveness of communication is measured by the subsequent actions, reactions, and behaviors. Addressing the right topic at the right time to the right person in the right way can yield amazing results. When working in groups, an inclusive message can bring people together and focus energy on the key objective. In order to do this, you must be able to reach your group. With many free options available, conveying an important message in a way that caters to the group need not be costly. Researching and comparing outlets may take time, but this is time well-spent finding a method that engages the majority. (I put emphasis on "majority" because it is next to impossible to find something that works for everyone. That said, you may have to use multiple formats to ensure that everyone is included in the communication.)

Appropriate Topics for Group Settings

For each correspondence drafted for dissemination to groups, the content and its presentation must be approached with careful consideration. Each component—Content, Context, and Conversation—reflects the purpose and meaning of the message shared with the recipients. Before the message is sent, measure the message for each of these components for clarity and correctness.

Content: What do you need to say?
For topics that can stir emotions, communicating in-person with an additional person present is best. Exchanges through electronic means can go awry, and if you believe there is a possibility of misinterpretation for the recipient or the sender, that the conversation should not continue in writing. At this point, some choose to include another party in the communication by showing them the message or, when responding, adding a third party as a recipient. This is not always helpful or appropriate. When evaluating how to respond, consider the topic. Is it a private or personal matter? Who is impacted by the outcome of the discussion or transmission of information? Did the use of formatting, punctuation, or emoticons contribute to the tone of the message? If the answers to any of these questions give pause, then the conversation should continue by phone or in-person, if possible.

Context: What is the setting? How is the environment?
Another consideration is the context of the transmission. The context can give insight to the method of communication utilized by the sender; it can also provide clues for how to respond and to whom. For example, if the correspondence is sent from management or supervisory personnel, it is not appropriate to respond in the presence (virtual or physical) of your coworkers or your subordinates. Each organization has a set hierarchy and established protocol for resolving conflicts or issues; the procedures should be followed without deviation except in instances where those who are in the position to respond fail to do so. It is important to demonstrate respect for the people in the organization and the systems in place by the organization at all times. If there are flaws in the systems, it is acceptable to bring to the attention of the appropriate personnel with positive suggestions and good intentions. At some point in your career,

you will face a hostile work environment and must successfully cope with it to avoid blemishes to your reputation and track record. The best way to cope is to document everything in writing. For conversations, follow it up with a message summarizing the conversation and asking the recipient for confirmation.

Conversation: Who needs to be included?

When you communicate in a group setting, you should address the group as such. It is not appropriate to call out individuals on their shortcomings or otherwise draw negative attention to any individual. There are direct and indirect ways to do this.

Transitional Conversations

Sometimes, group messages require one-on-one follow-up. When conversations get tense or participants become nonresponsive, it may be a result of a change in comfort level. Other times, a one-on-one conversation in progress develops a need for more participants. This need could come from the desire for additional expertise, from the requirement of objectivity, or simply from landing on a topic of interest for specific individuals. No matter the reason, a successful transition that does not offend or preclude any of the participants is needed. Some questions to consider prior to sending a message with multiple recipients include: who is it from; who/what is it about; who is currently involved; who needs to be involved; and what is the nature of the email?

If a conversation took place through any forum that contains threaded messages (e.g. instant messenger service, email), the contents of all the prior messages should be reviewed. Ensure the message contains nothing private or personal the current participant does not want shared. Ask the permission of the current participant prior to sharing the contents of the message. You can reply to the message and add the new participant as a recipient. If a verbal conversation took place over the phone or in-person, you can simply invite the person to join the conversation verbally. However, in the event there are physical or time barriers, you can initiate a written message that provides a brief summary of the conversation and send it to the new participant and include the current participant(s) on the message.

In email communication, individuals often misuse or abuse the "Forward," "Reply," and "Reply All" functions. The purpose of the "Forward" button is to share information with a new recipient. When a message is forwarded, it includes the attachments from the most recent message and the entire thread of messages. If some of this information should not be shared, then the message will need to be edited before it is sent. The major distinction for the "Reply" and "Reply All" functions is the recipient. To send a message to the sender only, use the "Reply" button; when the "Reply All" option is used, the sender and the original recipients receive the message.

Many email users also do not know the distinction between the carbon copy (CC) and the blind carbon copy (BCC) functions in email communication. These terms originated from the use of paper forms made of carbonized paper. The paper is usually a stack of three with the top page serving as the original copy and the subsequent pages being the "carbon copy" that is distributed to someone else and put away in storage, away from general public use. When individuals utilize these functions, this historical perspective should be considered for the purpose. To convey a clear message about the context and where the additional participant fits in to the conversation, one may need to change the subject line and add or remove attachments. All messages with attachments or information from previous messages should begin with a brief explanation of content and its relevance. Remove unnecessary information like email addresses and past messages.

A great way to transition between forms of communication is to ask. Any point the correspondence requires clarity or more time to exchange information is the opportunity to transition. Taking opportunity to transition to another setting or format for communication is a sign of respect for others' time and knowledge. To set aside a designated time for a topic, one should ask about the other party/parties' general availability and give them preference. In a group setting, recognizing when a discussion is going beyond the scope of the group's goals and objectives is very important. This may differ when moving from a group meeting to a small group with three or less group members. In a large group in the workplace, one should be considerate of heavy work times, holidays, break times, and other set meetings times.

When inviting others to meet at a designated time, the goal is to simplify the process. Start by offering at least three options. Those options should vary in day of the week (e.g. Monday, Thursday, and Saturday) and time of day (morning, lunchtime, late afternoon, or evening). It is acceptable to list these options as a numbered list inside the body of a message if the sender and the recipients are not using the same communication tools or software or if there is uncertainty about the level of technological expertise. If these factors are not obstacles, the group should use appointment scheduling technology that is compatible with a variety of systems. Many systems are built into other communication modes, like Microsoft Outlook, Google Calendar, and others. Also, many web-based applications are available for free like Doodle and NeedToMeet, and these allow participants to send a link to a poll using just a recipient's email address.

It is customary to send a reminder at least three days (or 72 hours) before a meeting is set to take place. A good technique is to use the original message and adjust the subject to begin with "REMINDER." Notifications can also be automated when using software or web-based applications. When disseminating information as a result from a meeting, be sure it is timely. The decisions could require action that needs to take place immediately while other information may be standard topics in which updates are provided. The rule-of-thumb is to send notes from the meeting to the group no later than a week after the meeting has concluded. This gives enough time for notes to be organized by the writer, reviewed by a second individual, revised by the writer and, finally, disseminated to the group.

Summary

Effective communication skills are valuable for career advancement and collaborative efforts in the workplace. This skill set not only helps to secure a job but also enables employees to maintain successful interpersonal relationships when working with others. The most important component of successful communication is courtesy and respect for people's expertise, time, and contribution. Nonverbal communication is a strong complement to verbal communication that happens in-person or through virtual means; due to technological advances, this nonverbal communication is still evident in written communication with the use of visual expressions such as emoticons and memes.

References

Attana, A., Raofb, A. H. A., Omarc, N. A. M., Izwan, K., & Abdullahd, M. H. (2012). Establishing the construct of workplace written communication. *Procedia - Social and Behavioral Sciences 66*, (2012), 76 – 85.

Baharun, R., & Suleiman, E. S. (2008). The employers' perceptions of what makes graduates marketable. *Contemporary Issues in Marketing.*

Canale, M., & Swain, M. (1980). Theoretical bases of communicative approaches to second language teaching and testing. *Applied Linguistics, 1*(1), 1-47.

Cardon, P. W., & Marshall, B. (2015). The hype and reality of social media use for work collaboration and team communication. *International Journal of Business Communication, 52*(3), 273-293.

Goudreau, J. (2013). How to communicate in the new multigenerational office. *Forbes Magazine.* Retrieved from: http://www.forbes.com/sites/jennagoudreau/2013/02/14/how-to-communicate-in-the-new-multigenerational-office/#71a7f7c750d8

Kinnick, K. N., & Parton, S. R. (2005). Workplace communication: What *The Apprentice* teaches about communication skills. *Business Communication Quarterly, 68*(4), 429-456.

Kudesia, R. S., & Elfenbein, H. A. (2013). Nonverbal communication in the workplace. *Nonverbal communication,* 805-832.

Media Platform. (2015). The History of Corporate Communications Technology. Retrieved from: https://www.mediaplatform.com/2015/06/history-corporate-communication-technology/

Patterson, M. (2012). *Nonverbal behavior: A functional perspective.* Springer Science & Business Media.

Robles, M. M. (2012). Executive perceptions of the top 10 soft skills needed in today's workplace. *Business Communication Quarterly, 75*(4), 453-465.

Staggers, J., Garcia, S., & Nagelhout, E. (2008). Teamwork through team building: Face-to-face to online. *Business Communication Quarterly, 71*(4), 472-487.

Thornbory, G., & White, C. (2007). How to... write reports effectively. *Occupationnel Health, 59*(2), 20.

Zehr, M. A. (1998). New office economy putting greater demands on schools. *Education Week, 17*(23), 7.

Marketing and Social Media

The Journey into Blogging
Carol Roberts

Social media is the way we communicate in our businesses as well as our personal lives. In truth, the entire World Wide Web has become a part of our daily lives. For people interested not only in marketing and business communication but also in information seeking and sharing, blogging has become one of the media many people use. Van Fossen (2005) noted in her very helpful post, "Blogs are giving people a voice they never had before."

Planning

There are two possible paths to take before starting to blog. One is to jump right in and learn along the way (as I did and am still doing); the other is to read blogs about blogging, take notes, and set up your blog after you have absorbed a lot of information. The trouble with the second approach is that it may seem like too much trouble. A surprisingly abundant supply of information is out there, especially on the Internet—from other bloggers' posts to sites like WordPress and Google Blogger. Another subject to investigate early on is that of key words. Matthew Kaboomis Loomis (2016) discusses this (and much more) on his blog *Build Your Own Blog*. Perhaps there is a middle ground: take a workshop, read a little, but do not worry about knowing everything before starting. This thought may be the most important one in this entire chapter.

Definition and Reason

The term "blog" is short for "Web-log," but the abbreviated form took over quickly, with the first known use of this word being in 1999 according to Merriam-Webster's Learner's Dictionary. A blog is a website designed usually by an individual but occasionally by a group or a corporation. It is a running series of posts listing the most recent at the top. The blogger may wish to share their interests with readers or promote their business. The point is that the blog is public information that the author can categorize so certain posts can be found by persons who search for that subject. For instance, I once wrote a post titled "To a Young Person Contemplating Suicide" on Poetry for the Journey and received a comment from a thankful reader who said they "must have been meant to see it." That comment was enough to inspire me to keep my blog running.

But what, exactly, is the difference between a blog and a web site? Lorelle Van Fossen (2005) summarized that a blog is more newsy and personal, a web site more static and serious. She admitted that even in 2005, however, this difference was becoming blurred.

In *Job Searching with Social Media for Dummies*, the author proposed another reason to blog. Waldman (2014) states:

> An added bonus of blogging? Employers who see you passionately turning out articles, videos, or slides in the area of your expertise will see that you're truly passionate about your work and have a depth of knowledge that may help their organization. Also, not many other candidates are brave enough to put themselves out there and share their voice. (p. 7)

For the potential blogger, Darren Rowse (2016) discussed 22 questions to help "pre-bloggers" decide if they are suited for this venture. He suggested asking questions such as "Am I a good communicator?" "Am I a self-starter?" "Am I organized?" "Am I social?" This blog post is continually updated and is one of the best resources for the new blogger.

Who, What, and Why?

Two important questions for the would-be blogger are what is the topic of your blog and who is the intended audience. Blogs are not journalism (impartial reporting) nor are they meant to be. They are the opinions and viewpoints of the writer (or business). Having a clear idea of your purpose before beginning is best. Remember: authors need to take their time to get focused— especially if you have several interests; does there need to be a separate blog for each passion, or could they coalesce? For instance, I was a Christian and interested in spiritual things, a writer and a poet, and interested in setting up poetry therapy groups. I started one blog through WordPress called Poetry for the Journey and another through Google called Life Story Solutions. As I progressed, I realized that I probably would be bringing all three—my faith, life story writing, and poetry— together. So, I kept the Poetry for the Journey title for my blog but added "Journal Writing: Write Your Story, Heal Your Life" on the front page. My other blog is still out there (because they never go away), but I am only posting to the one.

Further important questions are as follows:
- What are other people saying about your subject;
- What are other blogs with a similar interest;
- What does your potential blog bring that is unique;
- Who might be curious to read your blog; and
- Are you a member of an organization related to your passion?

Look for synonyms of your key words. For example, an author writing a blog concerning dachshunds used the term "wiener dog." She might have missed a lot of readers had she not realized the need to use the proper breed name. The above questions are also relevant when considering a possible name for your website. A vast amount of helpful information is available on the internet. Clearly, you will want to know what key words people search. (See Matthew Kaboomis Loomis' blog on this subject, referenced later.) This topic is huge, however, and is not something that needs to be mastered by the beginner. Getting your blog out there— i.e. able to be found when people search for a keyword similar to yours— can cost money. I decided I might need to start a new blog. I picked out a favorite title and checked it out on Google. It was already used. After trying this several times, I decided for the time being I would create a new Facebook page (which I had just realized I could do) and connect the blog to it so that readers would be redirected to my blog post.

Read the Experts

In May 2016 when I searched "blogs about blogging," the result that attracted me was "Top 25 Blogs about Blogging" on DailyBlogTips by Daniel Scocco, written in 2007. (He is now specializing in another related field but still co-edits DailyBlogTips). The last comment on this blog was in 2011, but I looked at several sites that were still helpful and relevant— ProBlogger, Quick Online Tips, DailyBlogTips, and Bloggers Blog. The most popular was ProBlogger. Darren Rowse is the founder and editor of ProBlogger Blog Tips and Digital Photography School and has a very thorough and helpful blog. This business of keeping up with the experts is ongoing.

Web Hosting Challenges

In June 2016, I was aware that my WordPress contract would be up in August and that I would have to make a decision about the hosting of my blog. I had not found the customer service at WordPress particularly user-friendly, although they do have many helpful tutorials. I was also looking for something a little cheaper. I called GoDaddy and had a good chat with one of their representatives, and in July I signed up. I love their helpful customer service, but in early August, I had a frustrating week as they dealt with problems on their end. After a week of not being able to update my new site, I called again and was walked through some temporary programming steps that got me up and running. August was a difficult month. Three times (the 1st, the 5th, and the 11th), I wondered whether I would be able to continue because of some technology glitch. Numerous times, I was on the computer or phone (sometimes for hours) with Geek Squad, GoDaddy, and Google. For example, when I thought my new site was ready and went to show it to a friend, an error message came up instead. I called GoDaddy twice, and their first-level consultants said, "We can see it from here." Finally, I called a third time and got transferred to a second-level consultant. He said that Google had caused my problem. My site was listed with an extra letter; instead of "http," it was "https." That one letter was sending my site out of orbit (and demanding that I pay more money, which was not necessary for my site.) The GoDaddy guy gave me step-by-step instructions, but I had to go on the Google site and do it myself. I included this story as an encouragement to be persistent when these glitches happen. They will happen, but there is always a solution.

Check Out the Neighborhood

As mentioned at the beginning of this chapter, a logical step in the journey to blogging is to first read other blogs. Do a Google search on your interest and see what comes up. This gives you an idea of what is already being blogged. If you like a site, follow or subscribe to it. It might help you focus on your own niche. Subscribing to other blogs was what made me realize that I had my own ideas and passions and that I, too, could blog. It gives you a great opportunity to learn what others are saying about your subject. Also, it saves you time as once you follow or subscribe to another blog, you automatically get notified every time they post. You will receive messages via an RSS reader. WordPress still provides this service of receiving the posts of blogs you follow; Google does not. You need to comment on a post if you can, leaving your own information (your specific URL address which you copy and paste from your actual web site) so they can answer your comment (and perhaps also generate some more interest in your blog). Of course, you will need to be a polite participant, only making comments if they are truly relevant and not overdoing it. On my Word Press blog, I can check my new mail, but I can also ignore it. It is my call.

A more advanced level of this phase of blogging is what Darren Rowse explained in his blog "7 Strategies for Growing Community on Your Blog": growing community. This is something to look forward to and hope for but is very difficult to do. It is when people not only comment on your blog but begin commenting on each other's comments. Some of Rowse's ideas for building community are to write in your own voice as if you were writing a letter to a friend; invite interaction by doing things such as asking a question, setting a challenge, or taking a poll; run projects and challenges; sponsor events (e.g. Rowse invited people to meet him in person at a London pub, and three people showed up.He continued to host the event, and he later sold 200 early-bird tickets for the meet-and-greet.); and put your readers in the spotlight. I highly suggest reading Rowse's blog.

Audience Response

Think about your desired response. The language for this is often "a call to action." In other words, at some point bloggers want to consider making money from their blog. If you offer a service and not a product, you will need to get creative. Can you offer a box to check or an opinion to share? I am setting up a Facebook page with the goal of offering to lead small writing groups. However, I have also written a memoir-writing workbook that friends have found helpful. My goal when I started this chapter was to offer my workbook for sale directly from my blog. I accomplished that goal in two months. At this stage, setting it up was success. I decided it might be time to call in someone with experience. Margaret Rode at Websites for Good (recommended to me by The Center for Journal Therapy) was wonderful. She can take people all the way from start to an up-and-running site finish, but I just needed help at the end. I told her how much money I could spend, and she took me on anyway and gave me way more than my money's worth! She did need my passwords, so be sure you know and trust your consultant before handing over such sensitive information.

If you offer a product, how will people pay you? PayPal has a solution. You will be asked to give your name (actual or otherwise). PayPal will then add it to your PayPal account to share with friends or customers. The payer clicks the link and enters the amount to pay, and PayPal takes care of the rest. You can set up a merchant account ahead of time with no cost, so even if you never offer anything to sell or take a while to do so, you will be ready. They are very easy to work with, too. Furthermore, when I bought a book to test my site, I learned how to refund. My mantra has pretty much been "Learn something new every day." That was such a day.

Once you have thought through your purpose, your intended audience (and you can get very specific about this), your title, and the possibility of sharing information and making money with your blog, it is time to begin.

Method

There is no simple set of steps to be taken in this project; you will always go back, edit, and/or change your mind. You might even start a blog and abandon it for lack of response or a lack of interest on your own part. But the very first decision you must make is who will host your blog. Blog services do this, sometimes for free and sometimes for a cost. WordPress is the most popular, and Google's Blogger is next. Watch videos on YouTube, read blog tutorials, and compare. Word Press has a support page where you can find numerous tutorials. There is a "Learn WordPress" section on their site, or you can go to the official WordPress Support page. I would recommend starting with WordPress—their web site and their hosting. I think the key to success in using

WordPress is to read their tutorials. GoDaddy is a little bit cheaper, but not much, insofar as web hosting is concerned. Google's Blogger has the reputation of being easier to navigate. You can watch Google Blogger's official YouTube channel and visit the Blogger Help Center. However, Google and WordPress are not the only ways to start a blog. Other web site starters and other web hosts do exist. Spend some time on the web and investigate the various options. In the end, you just have to decide and get started.

After you decide which service to use, the websites are very helpful. They will lead you through step by step. Of course, it helps that you have already chosen your title and thought about desired readership. Many sites offer help for writing ideas, but I have not struggled with ideas. Setting up a blog is a process, however. You have room to make changes. Once you do choose a site, you will be surprised at how easy it is to complete your first post. WordPress has a "Draft" feature with a preview button that allows you to see how your post will look on the site. This stage is where it gets exciting! There is something about seeing your own words (not to mention your chosen theme— design, colors, etc.) up there on the computer screen!

Managing Your Blog's Comments

Will you allow all comments, or will you require a stamp of approval before the comment is visible? Google has a set of instructions that leads you through this decision. This kind of step can be intimidating if you are new to this whole process. Basically, you sign in to Blogger (if that is your host) and to your blog. Select which blog to update if you have more than one. Look to the left of the screen where a number of choices are listed. At the bottom of the list is "Settings." Click on it. You will be led to another screen with several more choices. Click "Embedded" if it is not already done; as you look down on the screen, you will see something like "Who Can Comment." I decided that I wanted to approve comments before they are published. Click Save.

Making it Easy to Find You

Because you want your blog to be read, you can link your blog individually to people you know. You can use the social media sites such as Facebook and Twitter, generally known as microblogs. Frances Caballo (2015) has a good article on Linkedin about Twitter for writers. Search Engine Optimization, or SEO, makes your blog more visible based on the way you use key words. Google has a Search Engine Optimization Starter Guide, which I recommend. Learn more about descriptive titles, categories, tags, and labels to make your blog easier to find and navigate. This step does not need to be taken in the beginning stage. People use the shorter sites to promote their longer blogs as well as to communicate briefer messages more often. If you took my earlier advice, you will have already connected to some online communities. You can use Google Blog Search or Blog Catalog to search for more relevant sites. Many bloggers post links to other blogs. Go to the site you want to link, copy the URL address (the complete address, such as http://www.problogger.net/blog/), go to the "New Post" page on your administrative page, and paste the link. Done.

A Little More About Facebook and Blogging

As I thought about my goal of finding some women who might enjoy reading my thoughts about writing and healing, it occurred to me that I already have a community of women who connect with me on Facebook. I do not know all of them personally, but they each know others. In addition, they are— for the most part— in the Nashville area. I took a workshop on social media taught by The IMC Girl, and when we got to Facebook, I realized that I could start my own dedicated business page with the intent of reaching those women. As a further step, I paid $30 (six days for $5 a day) to boost my site. Facebook said that I reached over 10,000 people, mostly between 13 and 17! I also accomplished the task of doing a new thing on the journey.

You may find that microblogging will be sufficient for your needs: posting short articles, pictures, and videos with the purpose of connecting with a few (or several) friends. Go ahead and try the blog, but keep in mind that the options are out there for a more present, immediate experience. Moreover, so far as the future is concerned, ProBlogger says to be on the lookout for "social blogging," which will fill the cyber space between blogging and microblogging. There is no end to this journey.

References

http://learnersdictionary.com/

Blogger Getting Started Guide. (2016) Retrieved from
https://support.google.com/blogger/answer

Caballo, F. (2015). 7 reasons why twitter is awesome for writers.
LinkedIn. Retrieved from https://www.linkedin.com/pulse/7-
reasons-why-twitter-awesome-writers-frances-caballo

Loomis, M. K. (2016). *Using key words. Build Your Own Blog.*
Retrieved from
http://www.buildyourownblog.net/blog/keyword-research-
blog-niche/

Roberts, C. (2016). Write your story, heal your life. *Poetry for the
Journey.* Retrieved from http://poetryforthejourney.com/

Rowse, D. (2016). 7 Strategies for Growing Community on Your
Blog [Web log post]. Retrieved from
http://www.problogger.net/7-strategies-for-growing-
community-on-your-blog/

Rowse, D. (2016). 22 indicators to help you determine if you're
suited for starting a blog [Web log post]. Retrieved from
http://problogger.com/podcast/120-2/

Scocco, D. (2007). Top 25 blogs about blogging. *Daily Blog Tips.*
Retrieved from http://www.dailyblogtips.com/top-25-blogs-
about-blogging/

Tharpe, C. T. (2016). Is Facebook for you? *Facebook for Business
Workbook.* Nashville: NeuIMC.

Waldman, J. (2014). *Job searching with social media for dummies.*
Hoboken, New Jersey: John Wiley & Sons, Inc.

VanFossen, L. (2005). Learning about Blogging and How to Blog
[Web log post]. Retrieved from
https://lorelle.wordpress.com/2005/08/29/learning-about-
blogging-and-how-to-blog/

Writing an Effective Book Review in the 21st Century

Annie Laura Smith

Book Review History

The Atlantic published an article by Sarah Fay (2012) titled "Book Reviews: A Tortured History," in which Fay advised that since the 1800s "[l]amenting the state of the book review has been the literary world's favorite pastime." Other book authors and journalists through the years echoed this sentiment. This is due in a large part to the fact that book reviewers are not necessarily experts in the field of literature. However, by 2016, book reviews have evolved into a more comprehensive treatment of the respective book with Internet resources and guidelines available for in-depth reviews— whether the reviewer is an expert or not.

How to Become a Book Reviewer

How does one become a book reviewer? To get started, purchase books of interest from genres as given in Table 1, and publish reviews on open platforms such as those noted in Table 2. Book review blogs are given in Table 3. Search the Internet for additional sources. Many websites address reviewer requirements as well as offer opportunities to do reviews either by request or on assignment. Book review markets often require submissions of sample book reviews for evaluation before making an assignment. The reviewer is usually allowed to keep the book if the review is done as an assignment. Historically, book reviews were published in print media. The Internet now adds additional possibilities and reaches a larger audience.

Purpose and Content

Book reviews offer a critical assessment; their most important function is to act as a commentary, not merely a summary such as a book report. The role of the book reviewer is to advise readers about the merits and/or shortcomings of the book. It is a discussion of the basic strengths and weaknesses—this includes a relevant description of the book; its overall perspective, argument, or purpose; and a critical assessment of the content. This information addresses the organization, setting, dialogue, plot (for fiction), Table of Contents, illustrations, activities, glossary, and index (for nonfiction). Book reviews vary in content, but generally include the following information:

Fiction:

    Title
    Author and Illustrator
    Copyright Date
    Publisher
    Age range if a children's book
    ISBN
    Prices
    Word Count

Body:

    Setting— Note the setting and how it influences the story
    Timeline— Explain how the timeline affects the story
    Characterization— Note if there is good characterization that makes the characters believable.
    Challenges— Describe the challenges of the main character, and how these challenges are resolved.
    Point of View (POV) —Note if the Point of View is first or third person and if it shifts during the story.
    Plot— Observe if the plot is well developed and engaging
    Title of Series (if part of a series)
    Recommendations— Would you recommend the book to others? If it is a children's book, would school libraries want to order it or—if applicable— the series?

Author's Note— Does the author or publisher explain the author's background or provide other relevant information for the novel, chapter book, or picture book?
List other publications by this author whether in a Series or stand-alone titles

***Nonfiction:*

Title
Author and Illustrator
Copyright Date
Publisher
Age Range (if a children's book)
ISBN
Prices
Word Count

Body: (This may vary)

Introduction
Prologue
Table of Contents
Subheads
Illustrations
Activities
Glossary
Index
Title of Series (if part of a series)
Author's Note— Does the author or publisher explain the author's background or provide other relevant information for the book? List other publications by this author whether in a series or stand-alone titles
Recommendations— Would you recommend the book to others? If it is a children's book, is it age appropriate and would school libraries want to order it or—if applicable— the series?

Steps for a Review

Using efficient reading techniques by being a flexible and involved reader to provide an adequate review is essential. A flexible reader will vary their reading speed according to the type and difficulty of the material. An involved reader begins reading with a stated purpose to determine the quality of the assigned book and to write a review. These skills allow the reviewer to skim, scan, and get an overall picture of the content before actually reading a respective book.

A book reviewer should be an avid reader and in touch with the many book genres as listed in Table 1. Plan to take notes while reading and record pages for reference information. Book Reviews typically range from 500-750 words; specific guidelines will be given by the book review site.

For both fiction and nonfiction, begin with the cover and record the book title, author, and illustrator (if present). Turn to the publisher's page and record the copyright date, ISBN, prices, and word count. The prices and additional ISBN can also be found by searching the title on the web. Review the Table of Contents and note if the book is divided into sections or chapters. Identify the Glossary and Index for Nonfiction. Include if there is information on books and websites. Advise if there are related activities provided. Note if there are black and white or color illustration, sidebars, or other illustrative materials.

Drafts of a Review

Plan to go through several drafts of the book review in order to focus on important points. Include revealing quotations or notable facts to emphasize your observations. Strive to give an informative and insightful review. When the final draft is completed, use the notes taken earlier to go back to the original information in the book and check these data for accuracy.

Table 5.1
Book Genres

Action and Adventure
Anthology
Art
Autobiography
Biography
Children's
Comics
Cookbooks
Diaries
Dictionaries
Drama
Encyclopedia
Guide
Health
History
Horror
Journal
Math
Mystery
Poetry
Prayer Books

Religion, Spirituality, & New Age
Romance
Satire
Science
Science Fiction
Self Help
Series
Travel
Trilogy

Table 5.2
Book Review Websites

BookBrowse— your guide to exceptional books	http://www.bookbrowse.com
Book Rabbit—an online book community	http://www.facebook.com/book rabbit
Goodreads— an Amazon company	http://www.goodreads.com
Kirkus Reviews— a book review magazine	http://www.kirkus.com
Kirkus Indie Reviews— for self-publishers	https://www.kirkusreviews.com/indie/about
New York Times— a special newspaper section	http://www.nytimes.com
Pacific Book Review Service— distributed to numerous news sites	http://www.pacificbookreview.com
Powell's Book Store— daily emailed book reviews	http://www.powells.com
Prime Book Reviews— reviewing the world one book at a time	http://www.primebookreviews.com
Publisher's Weekly— international news website of book publishing	http://www.publishersweekly.com/
The US Review of Books— online book review site	http://www.bookreviews.guru/

Table 5.3
Book Review Blogs

The Indie Review
The Book Designer
Writer Beware
Omnivoracious
Publetariat
The New York Review of Books
Tara Lazar
Helping Writers Become Authors
Galleycat
Smashwords
Book Riot
The Write Practice
Jane Friedman
The Millions
The New Yorker: Page Turner
Quillblog

Book Review Format

Use this format for writing a draft of the book review.

Book Title

Author

Illustrations by:

Body of the Book Review:

> *Follow the suggestions earlier in the chapter for this review. Include Title of Series if book is part of a Series, and list the other books. Be aware of the differences between fiction and nonfiction reviews and include the respective data for each genre where appropriate in the review. The word count will be defined by the respective book review site.*

Include the review here:

Copyright date, Publisher, Age Range (if children's book), prices

Reviewer:

FORMAT:

> *If children's book – Picture book, Middle Reader, Young Adult*

ISBN:

> *Include all ISBN 10 and 13 numbers*

Word Count:

References

Book reviews (2016). Retrieved from
http://writingcenter.unc.edu/handouts/book-reviews
February 23, 2016.

Fay, Sarah (2012) Book reviews: A tortured history. *The Atlantic*.
Retrieved from
http://www.theatlantic.com/entertainment/archive/2012
/04/book-reviews-a-tortured-history/256301/ June 27,
2016.

How to write a book review. (n.d.) Retrieved from
http://www.writingworld.com/freelance/asenjo.shtml
February 23, 2016.

List of book types or genres. (n.d.) Retrieved from
http://reference.yourdictionary.com/books-
literature/different-types-of-books.html June 27, 2016.

Brizee, A. (2016). Writing a book review. *Owl Purdue Online
Writing Lab.* Retrieved from
https://owl.english.purdue.edu/owl/resource/704/1
February 23, 2016.

The following resources provided by the UNC Writing Center –
Chapel Hill offer excellent information:

Drewry, J. (1974*). Writing Book Reviews*, Retrieved from
http://jirfp.com/in/jirfp/book_review.

Ohage, J.O. (Ed.). *(1987). Literary reviewing.* Charlottesville:
University Press of Virginia.

Teitelbaum, H. (1998). *How to Write Book Reports*. 3rd ed. New
York, NY: Macmillan.

Walford, A.J. (Ed.). (1986) *Reviews and reviewing: A guide.*
Phoenix, AZ: Oryx Press.

Fiction Writing and the World of Self-Publishing

Kristen Billingsley

Introduction

The End. You have anticipated this moment for as long as you can remember. To write the final words of your beloved novel is the most refreshing feeling any writer can have. After many months or years of pounding away on your keyboard, creating worlds and developing characters, you can finally take a breath— or can you? Writing an entire novel is not the end of your journey, but rather the beginning of your new career.

Deciding to publish your book is a scary thing! You have decided to allow potentially millions of people to read your written work. Today, with the beauty of technology, you have wonderful options. In bygone eras, to be taken seriously as an author, you had to be published traditionally, but now you can decide to self-publish— and your work looks just as lovely as the books that came out of the Big Five publishing companies.

Imaging that after doing the necessary research, you have opted to self-publish. Maybe you are the type of person who likes to have control over your work. You want all of the royalties, not just the 10%; you do not want to give up your rights to the book. You want to make the important decisions in editing and cover art. Or, perhaps you are the type of person who writes because it makes you happy and you want to share it with the world, but you do not want to be confined to deadlines, either. Whatever the reason, self-publishing seemed to be the best fit for you, and now you are ready to make it happen.

When you decide to self-publish, you have many things to keep in mind. The most important thing you must remember is that you, and only you, are responsible for everything. Everything that a publishing company does and pays for is now in your hands. Do not fret! It is not necessarily a terrible thing, or expensive. Given that you do your research and hire out the right team, it can be the most rewarding and fun part of publishing.

Hiring an Editor

The first and most important person on your publishing team that you should hire is your editor. Many people believe that the perk of self-publishing is that you can upload whatever and however many times you need, should you come across an error. That is true, but any reviews you get from having low-quality published work will stay with your book forever. Therefore, you should hire an editor before anything else; one could even go as far as to say to not even advertise your release date until you have done so. Why? Because if your book needs more work than you have time, then you have already put yourself in a pinch.

Editing has many different types, and essentially you should know about them all so that you have a clear idea for what you are paying. You also may not need to pay for certain editing services, depending where your strengths lie; however, no matter what, *always* pay for a line edit and at least two proofreads. So what are some of the different types of editing?

Content editing

Content editing— aka developmental editing— is when the editor goes over your plot, character development, pacing, descriptions, and your over-all storyline. Basically, anything that is not grammatical. This is a very useful edit for someone who may be writing for the first time, someone who may be entering into a new genre, or someone who feels like they are lacking in one of those areas. While this edit is very much worth the money, content editing is one of the few that you could get away with not having.

Line editing and copyediting

One of the most essential types of editing is the line edit or even a copy edit. A copyedit covers grammar and punctuation. That is it. The editor may comment on a major plot hole or inconsistency, but their main focus is the grammar. A line edit will not only clean up the writing, but also point out any issues. It is not as in depth as a content edit by itself, but if your writing is pretty well rounded, then you can skip the developmental and substitute it out with a good line edit to catch any unwanted straggling inconsistencies in the story.

Proofreading

Proofreading is always going to be a must. If your grammar and writing is spot on, then you can skip a line editor all together and go straight to the proof reader; however, the book must be up to par. A proofreader's job is to look for basic errors in spelling, grammar, and punctuation. It should not substitute your editor by any means. Because proof readers are basically looking for a needle in what should now be a pretty clean haystack, paying for two proofs by two different, proud editors is always a good idea. This way, you know that your work is nearly flawless by the time you publish.

Several editors are out there, and shopping around for the best one in your genre is crucial. You would not want a science fiction editor to look over your mystery thriller. Being on two different spectrums, they might not know all the rules associated with a genre in which they are not an expert. Compare prices for your list of editors to ensure you are getting a fair deal. You can even check out books that they have edited, and read them to see their quality of work. Most importantly, have at least two or three different editors. Sometimes during the busy publishing months, an editor may be too tied up and may have to put you on a long waiting list. If it does not work with your deadline, at least you have someone else you could turn to.

At the end of the day, you are responsible for putting out good quality work—especially if you plan on making money off of it. Out of every area that you will spend money on, editing is the one that you should not skimp on.

Choosing a Cover

Another area where you may spend some cash will be the first thing your readers ever see— your book's cover. Too many times you have heard "don't judge a book by its cover," and yet you gravitate to the first book that catches your eye externally. There is a good reason for it, too! The book cover should tell you the genre and at least some of the content in one glance.

If you are really good at Photoshop, then you could spend money on stock art or even take your own photos and put together a nice detailed cover. If this is the rout you plan on taking, then be sure to remember that a book cover is basically multimodal writing. Every detail, down to the font, should be intentional and give a visual art to what is inside the book. If you plan on creating your own, try several different mock ups and let a few people look at them so you know what is working. Creating the book cover could be just as daunting as writing the novel.

If you are not as talented or cannot even touch Photoshop with a ten-foot pole, hiring a graphic designer will be the best route. Like the editor, you should research each designer and compare their past work and prices. Find out exactly what the regulations are to commission them. Sometimes, designers will have different rules on what you are allowed to use the art for. This is something good to know upfront if you want to use your cover art on something other than the book.

Your graphic designer may even turn into an essential part of your team. Depending on what services they offer, they may make your posters, business cards, book marks, and many other pretties to promote your titles. Many graphic designers will even work alongside your interior book designers, which we will be covering next, to make your interior just as beautiful.

Designing the Interior

One of the final needs for your book is for it to be either set up for print or uploaded as an ebook. You can hire an interior book designer or even do it yourself. No matter which you choose to do, ensure that the format is clean, easy for the eyes to digest, and professional looking. Most publishing platforms— be they CreateSpace or Lightening Source for print, or Kindle Direct Publishing, Apple, or Smashwords for ebooks— have an easy to follow guideline that you can use straight out of Microsoft Word or Apple Pages.

Customizing your book with chapter heading designs and other art could make your book stand out even more. If you decide to customize your book, find out what font your cover artist used to make your book more consistent. Also, using art that is on the cover will help tie in the overall branding of your book. A simple logo or font could be what readers associate with your series. That extra branding in your interior could lead to more sales in your overall series.

Publishing Vendors

Once you have your book edited, a cover established, and your interior formatted, you are ready to publish. That means you have to decide what platforms you want to publish on, and you have plenty of options. Your major outlets will be Amazon, Barnes and Noble, and Apple. If you do not want to take the time to go through each outlet individually, you could always go through Smashwords or Direct 2 Digital. They offer a service to upload at all retailers for you—for a cut of the royalties, of course.

Another option you may have is to go through Amazon exclusively. Kindle Select gives you a few upper hands. Your books will be able to go through Kindle Unlimited (KU), a service where readers pay a subscription to all KU books. You will get paid from a percentage of the book being read. Your books will also be available in the Kindle Owners Lending Library (KOLL). This allows your book to be lent out to other readers by the purchaser. Like KU, you get paid by the pages read on KOLL.

Choosing the best publishing route for yourself is important, because it is one of the biggest marketing decisions you will make for your book. Scope out your genre on each outlet to see if a majority of your market is purchasing on a certain platform. Knowing where your audience is could determine how your sales will rise or fall.

After Publication

After you have published, you can sit back and watch the money flow in, right? You would be wrong, again. Truth of the matter is, e-publishing has become widely popular and, because of such, is extremely watered down with books. You will need to do more than just hitting a button to push your book into the view of readers. This is where marketing and branding comes into play.

Online Marketing
Social media, love it or hate it, could put your book in front of your main audience. With plenty to choose from— Facebook, Twitter, Google+, etc.— you can be on them all or you can be on just one; however, you must remember two things. One, be sure you are at least on the site that your readers are most active on. If your audience mainly sticks to Twitter, then be sure to be on there. If you have a big audience on Facebook, then be active on Facebook. You would not get many clicks to your books if you pushed your books down the throats of people who would not read your genre. Second, be active on the sites that you are on. If you are not someone who logs into social media often for your

own personal use, then this one might be tougher. Some people may create a Facebook page or Google+ account and completely forget about it. For readers who are actively searching you out, this would not be a good thing. For starters, they may believe you are abandoning your career and no longer wish to continue publishing. Giving little updates on your social media can put them at ease that more is coming. Also, social media is a good way to update your viewers on new works coming out or events you have coming up. With sharing features, your fans may even do all the hard advertising for you as they will share your posts and make your name a brand. Never underestimate what power social media can have over your sales.

Blog tours have been on the rise more recently and have many benefits for authors. For self-published authors, it may be hard to spend all the money to go to individual book stores and do signings. Why should you, when you have the power of the Internet? The best thing about blog tours is that they plaster your titles everywhere. This is a great thing! Like with social media, it burns your brand into the mind of readers. You will become more recognizable. While it may not generate sales immediately, it pushes for a long-term affect. Readers may see your book on a blog but not intend to buy it at the moment. A week later, they are searching on Amazon and come across your book. Immediately, they remember seeing it on a blog and decide they want to purchase it. Branding is key for these types of sales, and blog tours really can get the job done. Blog tours are also handy for search results. The more blogs your book is on, the better chance you have to be found on the first page of search results. This is extremely important as it gives you more discoverability— which is another huge part of branding. Blog tours can be fun, time consuming, and most of all, if done right, worth it.

Attending Conventions
While you may not be able to afford to set up a bunch of signings, it could be worth looking into participating in at least one

convention every year. There are tons of conventions aimed at readers and authors alike. Not only will you get to meet your current fans, and hopefully make some new ones, you also learn a lot by mingling with the other authors. Like always, it will be important to choose a convention aimed at your genre. If you are a Fantasy author, you would not want to go to a Contemporary Romance convention.

If you decide to participate in a convention, do not forget to look for swag to give away. You can choose from bookmarks, posters, magnets, mints, buttons, and so many more options to give away to your fans and future readers. Again, this is one of those times where you might not sell a lot of books, but you could set yourself up for future sales— it is about branding. What could you give to your readers that will not only place your titles on their mind but also could potentially be seen by their friends? Many authors will get even more creative and give away things that are themed throughout their book or series such as stick on tattoos that a character has. Ultimately, you do not want to leave the convention not having given any impressions. Then, you would be wasting your money.

There are tons of other marketing and branding strategies for authors down to giveaways, mailing lists, and local events. No matter what you do to promote your work, always be thinking of the audience. If you want to do more than just press a button and have your books sit on a virtual shelf, then you should remember that, in the end, you are your own publicist when you are self-published. It will take effort to get your book onto e-readers.

Being a Publisher and a Writer

Now that you have the self-publishing down, it is time to juggle being your own publisher and your own boss. The hardest thing about self-publishing is that *you* are in control of your own schedule. For a lot of writers, this is difficult, because we are spontaneous and procrastinators; however, if you expect writing to turn into a career, you cannot have a two-year turnaround these days. Unlike before e-publishing, fiction readers gobble up books, and if you wait too long, they will forget all about you and move on to the next author. By the time your next book is released, the reader may not even remember you at all. Good luck with having them come back around to purchase the next book. Coming up with a plan on the length between your books and how to stay on schedule is beneficial.

Always be Writing
The best way to stay on schedule is to always be writing. This is easier said than done. Many writers have a daily "peak time" for the best writing. This is the time when writing comes easiest to you and you are less likely to find yourself in a dreaded writer's block. For some, it is in the morning when they first wake up, others in the afternoon or evening, and then there are the night owls who do all of their writing while the other birds sleep. Find out when your peak time writing is, because that is when you will be able to push out the words quicker and more efficiently.

Of course, this is all to say that you are able to write during your peak time. The biggest problem is that while you are focusing on your writing career, you also have to make money somewhere else; or you may even have a bigger obligation—thus taking up your schedule during your best writing time. For many, this problem will become a career breaker. How do you write when you do not have time? If you are truly serious about being a full-time author or just wanting to write in general, you will make the time. It may not always be in your most optimal writing time, but even if you can crank out 300 to 500 words, it will be better than nothing. Find that little nook in a cranny time that you will be able to write even the smallest amount of words and do it. It could be on the bus on the way to work, during your break, or while your kids take that 15-minute nap. Many writers find that once they start writing, they cannot stop. Depending on what is next on your busy schedule, writing may even take priority, and you pop out more words than you expected to. So while you may not always be able to write during your peak time, always be writing; it will help your head stay in the game, and your word count will always increase.

Defeating Writer's Block
Even for the writers who stay on the strictest schedule, many will still always run into their biggest villain—writer's block. Writer's block drains authors of their creativity, sucking their ideas from their head like a tick. While this enemy is the most annoying, authors can overcome it by jotting down some ideas, writing an insert, or even just by leaving it alone.

Jotting down some ideas can defeat the torment of writers block. Many writers choose to free write and just write whatever pops in their head. Some like to create webs and connect their ideas together. Whichever or whatever your preferred method is to get your ideas on paper is—do it. Not only will it help clear the mind, but you will keep focused on the project itself. As you continue to place ideas on paper, you will begin to see clearly the next move to make and the light at the end of the tunnel for writers block.

Sometimes, the cause of the block is because you get stuck at the beginning, but you know exactly where you want to go at the end. Writing an insert could be just the cure you need, so go ahead and write the ending! No one said you had to write linear. This tactic not only helps you write your idea before you forget it but also, by the end of the insert, you could be bubbling with ideas on what to write in the beginning to pull it together.

Another way to kick writer's block in the butt is to simply leave it alone. This, of course, goes against the keep writing method, but sometimes stepping away is needed as writers become stressed from over-contemplating their ideas. You can overthink and not get anywhere. Instead, if you were to take a step back and do another activity, then the block could be eased. Listen to music;

go on a walk; for those who paint, paint; or, if you are a TV junkie, watch an episode or two of your favorite show. While it is important not to stay away from your writing for too long, doing something else may jog an idea from your mind or give you the needed break to get back on your path of creativity.

Whatever your method may be, find a way to defeat writer's block. It may be the only thing standing in your way to becoming a full time author, as a writer's block can prevent you from staying on schedule with your new deadlines. Remember, keeping your schedule and always writing should be top priorities. You do not have time to let writer's block stand in your way.

Avoiding Burnout
There is another enemy that might try to sneak up on you in the self-publishing world—the writing burnout. As opposed to writer's block, you know how you want your story to go, and you know the words that you need to put down on the paper; the problem is actually having the willpower to do it. Burnout is usually caused by one of two reasons. First, you are pouring all your energy into trying to "make it big" to the point that you just want to give up. Second, you have actually made it as a full-time author, and all the work that goes along with it has left you mentally dry. In either case, you have ways to overcome burnout.

If you are stuck on the idea that you might become the next J.K Rowling or even self-published extraordinaire Hugh Howey, then this could definitely burn you out quickly. It is a pipe dream that only a very small percentage actually get to live. Notice how there is always one series or author that is talked about for the year or even a decade? Now, think about how many authors are publishing every single day. While hitting the top of the reading charts is not completely impossible, it is highly unlikely that you will be the single author to become the talk of the entire world. Instead of focusing all of your energy on an idea of becoming the next author sensation, focus on the stories you are writing.

For most fiction authors, the reason you write is because the story is itching away like a bug and will not go away until the story is written. Allowing yourself to get wrapped up in the story allows your mind to be focused on the creative side of writing versus the business side of writing. When your energy is focused on being creative and allowing the story to take over, you are less likely to drain yourself of motivation as opposed to when you are driven by the idea of making a lot of money. Do not give up on the idea that you can become a full-time author, because you can. It is actually more in your favor to become a full-time author when you are driven by your stories, because your mind will be in the right place. Sure, you might not become a celebrity author, but if you could pay your bills and write full-time it would be worth it.

What if you already pay your bills with your novels, but have emptied yourself of your productivity? Many authors have found that once they have made a true career of their writing, it becomes harder to maintain their creativity for several reasons. One reason might similar to why you cannot write when you are trying to make it: you just get too wrapped up in the self-publishing business. Another reason could be that you are listening to your fans too much. Half of your fans want one thing, and the other half wants something completely different. Or maybe, you are a power author who has nearly 100 plus books out, and the thought of writing is just mundane. Sure, you could try and put all your energy towards the story itself rather than the business, but chances are you just see writing as work and no longer exciting. Stories are just not popping out at you like they did before. When this happens, you may need to take a step back and allow your writing muse to return to you.

Because writing has become your source of income, it might be scary to take a break, but this is also the most important reason to do so. If your visionary drive does not return, your readers will catch on and your sales will dwindle. First, you should have some money put back in your savings for a hard month or two. While your sales will hopefully continue to profit income while you are on hiatus, you would not want to take the chance that you end up in a financial rut. Depending on your savings could determine how long you can afford to be away from writing. It could be a few weeks, a month, or maybe— if you can truly afford to— several months. You do not want to stay away too long, but you want to give yourself enough time to find your source of imagination.

During your time away from writing, do not become a couch potato. Instead, do things that are meaningful to you. Chances are you have been neglecting other things you love in life to dedicate your time to writing. Go out and do them! Is it spending time with family or friends? Traveling? Maybe you have not read a book in over a year, because you just did not have the time? Often, we get so caught up in the fact that we are making money writing that we do not want to lose it. So, we stray away from all of these things we enjoy, and it causes our work to become fruitless, unimaginative, and dry. Once you have restored balance in your life, your mind might open up to new possibilities. Who knows? You might even find creative light in a new genre!

While you are away from writing, you do not want to completely leave the scene. This could make it harder to want to return when you have so much fun not writing. Stay connected with your fans. You do not have to be pimping your latest work to reach out to them. While you may have been listening to their wants a little too much before, now you are getting to know them. You realize just how much they love the worlds you create. This could be enough to reignite that artistic surge. While also staying connected with your fans, keep in touch with other authors. Authors really help pep each other up. There is just something about seeing someone else succeed that gives you an impulse to succeed. So, reach out to them and go to an author convention or a writers' group; chances are, when you see them typing away a great story, your instincts to create will kick back in as well.

Final Words

At the end of the day, writing should be something you want to do because you thrive on it. It should not be just a means of income. While paying your bills doing something you love is nice, making money without any emotional connection is tragic. While there may be a few exceptions, readers usually know when someone's heart is not in their work. There is always something a little extra or exhilarating about a fiction writer who is truly soaking up the addiction of writing a good story. If you are a fiction writer who has decided to self-publish, do not allow the enormity of everything you have to put into it— editing, marketing, etc.— discourage you from putting your work out there for others to read. Even if you do not pay your bills, writing alone can be an outlet to happiness. More importantly, as an author, stay focused to your work rather than attached to the business. While you want to maintain a prompt schedule, you do not want the business to take over your life. This could give the opposite effect and exhaust you. Self-publishing for a fiction writer should be about getting the stories of their worlds or characters out to the public. The fiction stories that are the most successful are the ones that pull readers into a world they could not have imagined— because you are the only person who did. So, continue to write, continue to create worlds, and continue to tell the stories of characters. Put your novel out for the world to read and connect to, but do not be afraid of the industry.

Business Writing

Grant Writing:
Crafting a Sales Pitch through Words
Tavia Garland

Many nonprofits depend on grants to fund their services and programs. A grant proposal is essentially a sales pitch for the non-profit: the grant writer's goal is to convince the funding foundation why the organization you represent is the best choice for the funding award. Grants are the life line of many non-profits; without grants, non-profits are extremely limited in what services and programs they are able to provide to their audience. Grant writing is an area of writing that can be quite lucrative, providing a more regular income for writers than other avenues. Grant writing consists of both basics and specific articles and information needed in most cases for each one, so, in essence, you have a simple formula to start with each time.

A grant proposal is both a sales pitch and a small, specific business plan rolled into one document, so while fact-based in design, some flair will help catch the attention of those challenged with reviewing each proposal and choosing the best organization for the award (Dees, et al., 2002, p.15). In many cases, these reviewers will read hundreds of proposals. Some sections of the proposal are specifically designed to be read first, as a preview. Grant proposals are created using an almost scientific method, much like research papers. While grant writing may not be the most creatively fulfilling genre of writing, the financial benefit can often help sustain the other projects the writer wishes to pursue.

How do I know all of this? Mostly through my own personal experience. I enjoy creative fictional writing much more than grant writing, but I quickly discovered I would have a hard time making ends meet relying solely on creative writing to pay the bills before I have a New York Best Seller (which has not happened as of yet). I was first introduced to grant writing as a possible career when I was working on my Master's Degree in Non- Profit Management and Leadership. Near the beginning of the program, I took a class focused on grant writing. I knew that non-profits used grants to fund programs, but that was all. I had no idea that both government funded grants and independent-foundation funded grants existed for organizations. During the class, I learned the basic components present in most grants and how to take that formula and create an eye-catching proposal. Of course, the grants in class were hypothetical, so I could tailor the descriptions to meet whatever program I wanted. This practice was much easier than working with a real grant, but the basics are the same. Since then, I have worked as a grant writer on a freelance basis for different organizations as well as now serving on the Finance Committee for the Carnegie Writers, Inc. I have managed my own 501(c)3 Non-Profit organization for a little over five years, and I oversaw the grants for that organization as well. This chapter is by no means an all-encompassing document regarding grant writing, but it will help you understand the basic structure and goals.

What Are Grants?

Various corporations and organizations offer grants— or, a sum of money to be used in a specific fashion— to assist non-profit organizations. A grant proposal is a sales pitch to a foundation describing why a certain non-profit is the best choice for the money available. According to the text Karsh and Fox (2014), grants can be awarded as one-time lump sums or as recurring deposits to the non-profit (p.27). Each of these will have different on-going requirements from the foundation, and certain situations will call for one more than another. If an organization is starting a new program from the ground up, then a lump sum grant may be more beneficial because of the initial start-up costs.

If the organization is planning on hiring a long-term employee to manage a program with low overhead, then a recurring grant may be a better option for the employee's salary. Considering 90% of the workforce in a non-profit is generally volunteers, salaries represent a very small number of applied for grants (Young, 2007, p.38). Most are for program costs, and those can vary greatly from organization to organization depending on what type of program is being implemented.

While an organization has to achieve non-profit status before applying for grants, many non-profits use the grants to expand or enhance services. Non-Profit status is a tax classification of an organization, basically stating that any donations made are tax deductible and the organization will now be held to standards of reporting outlined by the federal code for non-profits. A small reminder: labeling an organization as "non-profit" does not mean there is no profit on the books and tax returns (Hall & Howlett, 2003, p.87). This label means the profits are used within the organization to further the mission and not given to shareholders. No one benefits solely from the proceeds, like in a private business setting. Many large non-profit organizations will report large profits on their tax paperwork, but that money must be put back into the organization in some manner. Due to the transparency in financial reporting for non-profits, this is easier to track than with for-profit business. A small non-profit will have a small donor base, and will need more cash flow in some manner.

As mentioned previously, there are different ways to work on grant proposals. Some writers prefer to be freelance writers and work on grants for many different organizations on a case-by-case basis. Some of the larger and more established non-profits will employ grant writers on either a part-time or full-time basis with an hourly salary. When a writer is doing freelance work, they will generally receive an agreed-on amount of the grant upon award and receipt by the organization. This is typically 3-4% depending on the situation. 3-4% may not sound like much, but on a $50,000 grant, it comes to a nice sum of $1,500 to $2,000.

The issue some grant writers have when first starting is that there may be a six month to a year lag time between preparing and submitting the proposal and receiving the payout. On the other hand, acquiring a full-time hourly position working on grants without a track record of successfully awarded grants or a higher level degree in Non-Profit Management can be difficult, and these positions often do not pay more than an entry-level salary. After learning this, why would anyone chose to pursue this field?

Grant writing is a socially rewarding form of writing; non-profits need these grants to succeed with their implemented programs. People who are passionate about writing can use their skills and talent to give back to the community. A great satisfaction comes from working on a dynamic and impactful proposal and then watching the non-profit actually put the grant into effect as intended. In some cases, these grant awards can create jobs for people in a local community. For example, I worked for Pet Community Center in Nashville, Tennessee. This is a booming non-profit focused on spaying and neutering animals in the community, as well as providing convenient and low cost care for pets in the city. A grant through a much larger organization created a position at Pet Community Center paying $30,000 for two years—guaranteed funding so long as the program's requirements were met. The person in this position was to be a community liaison with targeted zip codes in an area from which most animals in trouble came. After six months of implementation, the number of intakes at the local animal shelter dropped by 10%, which means 10% fewer animals were euthanized in Nashville in the given timeframe. For me, this is a very tangible reward from working on this grant: actual lives were saved. Even in a field like grant writing where there is payment for successful proposals, there still needs to be an altruistic attitude to truly be happy working in the field.

How is grant writing different from other forms of writing? The purpose and intent is different from the beginning— grant proposals are more of a sales pitch than anything else. Grant writing is a combination of creative and documentary writing. Many writers adore creative writing in various forms, but the road to sustainability solely from writing is long and hard. Grant writing is a bit of a compromise: while not as creatively rewarding, there is a higher potential for financial gain as well as a means to still work on the creative projects simultaneously.

Getting Started

Grant proposals are academic in nature and heavily research-based. This can be a challenge if you are a freelancer writer with minimal previous experience with the non-profit (Wason, 2004, p.4). You need to know a few fundamental elements about an organization before beginning the initial research for a particular grant. The first two are the mission and vision of the organization. The vision is a broad spectrum statement regarding the organization, what its major goals are, and why the organization exists. The mission is a statement regarding plans to bring the vision to reality, the target audience, and service areas. These two statements will share a wealth of knowledge regarding the organization. The third element to investigate is the history of the organization including how long they have been working in the community, what programs have succeeded, and what has failed. Has the organization grown quickly and dramatically, or slowly over an extended period of time? If the non-profit is new, there may not be much to these questions, but the founders may be able to provide some back story, at least. If the vision, mission, and history are muddy and unclear, writing a grant proposal for the organization may be more challenging.

The next step is essential: learn about the grant. What is this specific grant's purpose? What will the organization do with the funding, and what will the ideal program look like? This is what you will write the grant proposal to describe; having a strong understanding here makes writing the proposal much easier and will result in a better proposal. If possible, meet with the Board of Directors, other leaders in the organization, people who volunteer within the programs, and anyone else who would have unique insight into the organization. This also provides a link to the organization to understand their style. For the leaders to approve the proposal for submittal, the soul of the non-profit has to be embodied in the grant. This step takes the grant from an average proposal to something that will stand out to the committee reviewing it. Research is essential throughout the whole process, as a grant proposal is a form of academic writing. Facts must be correct or the grant could be denied or revoked.

Gathering Information

As a whole, the process of gathering information can seem quite daunting. Some grant writers prefer to look at one section at a time when preparing to begin; otherwise, it can seem like too much information to adequately process. The most important step is to define the project. The research mentioned in the above section should provide most of the information needed for this portion. If not, then more research should be done before beginning the proposal. There are many defined sections that almost all grants require, so after the first few grants, you will have a much better idea of what you need up front.

The first step in defining the grant is to concretely decide what the goals of the grant request include. The whole purpose of the proposal is to tell the reviewing committee exactly where the money will be spent. Depending on the grant type, these goals may be specific or more abstract. The grant information and requirements usually outline how much detail is needed, and the amount of detail required will depend on if the grant is for a specific program. An example would be a $30,000 grant for after school programs in Metro-Nashville for tutors to assist students whose families have incomes below $40,000. In this case, a grant would specifically service this audience, so the programs would be very similar in all of the proposals. A non-specific example could be something as general as $15,000 for academic institutions to implement academic improvement programs for students. This could be a science program, an after -school program, or even a music program. The initial research with the organization will lead you to which direction the goals are heading. Even when there are non-specifically defined grant requirements, the goals in the final draft should be as specific and detailed as possible.

Once the goals have been defined, the next step is the funding source: the organization or foundation offering the grant. If you are freelance, some organizations will already have the grant they wish to apply for researched; however, many will contract the grant writer to also find grants for which the program would be eligible. Working for one organization on the payroll will almost always result in the grant writer researching and finding grants as part of their position (Thompson, 2003, p.22). Once the funding source has been identified, the time has come for more research. If this is the first time working with a funding source, I suggest attempting to make contact with them. A wealth of knowledge is available in some cases, including technical assistance, how the grants will be reviewed, the process the grant proposal will be put through, etc. While not every organization will be willing to answer these questions, you can typically make some form of contact with a project office or project manager. This initial contact can prove beneficial later; if questions arise, a relationship already exists between you and the organization, which can make the process much easier.

The most tedious portion is acquiring the guidelines of the grant. A few elements are present for all grants and are important to know at the beginning of the process. Some of this information may have been given in the step before if you were able to make direct contact with the organization or foundation supplying the grant. A basic list of need-to-know information includes deadlines, eligibility requirements, budgets, and whether there are multiple levels of awards granted or only one grant. Anyone wanting to write a grant proposal should not let the fact that a deadline for submittal is twelve months away lead to procrastination. This delay will add to your stress when crunch time comes, and the proposal will be of higher quality with adequate time allowed for research and preparation. Another helpful hint is to check the requirements on a regular basis: these do change on occasion, and the proposal may need to be adjusted. The most common change is a timeline extension, so it is usually in the grant writer's favor, but other modifications can happen as well. Once this gathering process is complete, it is time to put all of the information into the proposal form.

The Narrative

The first section is the Narrative, a critical component of the grant proposal. Many writers will draft a Narrative and then revise it once the proposal is complete. It must be compelling and persuasive. This is essentially the *why* section of the proposal and includes what is called "A Statement of Need" (Bray, 2013, p.5). The goal of the statement is to convince the reviewing committee that your organization is the best choice for this grant. The Narrative is often the first read section, as well, and will set the tone for the rest of the proposal. If the reviewing committee is not impressed by the Narrative, then they may not seriously review and consider the proposal.

The approach to the Narrative will vary from writer to writer, and this is the portion where the most personality will be seen. One success hint would be to use key names and people from the organization as much as possible as a resource; these people are directly connected to the grant and help support the idea that if this organization is chosen, people involved will make sure the grant is used well. The Narrative will be re-worded many times, to be as compelling as possible. The method for accomplishing the goals is often outlined here and, in many cases, will be supplied by the organization that wishes to obtain the grant. The writer's job is to then rework the statements to be detailed and vividly described without being wordy. This can be a challenge, especially at first, but focusing some time into this section will pay off immensely at the conclusion of the project.

Method of Evaluation

The "Method of Evaluation" will mostly come from the organization if the grant writer is freelancing, simply because someone who does not work with the organization on a regular basis will not have the knowledge needed to answer the questions (Thompson, 2013, p.38). However, the more a writer learns about the organization and the methods by which the proposal will be evaluated, the better the proposal will be; the more a writer knows, the more they are able to explain. The evaluation section must have a strong connection with the goals and objectives of the project. Specifics in this section are necessary, such as how many people will be helped by this grant or how many programs can be launched with this sum. An important factor to include is how the results will be measured—if there will be satisfaction surveys, data from outside sources, or other methods. One example for this would be the aforementioned grant given to Pet Community Center in Nashville. The grant was awarded based on the goal of lowering the animal shelter intake by 10% in the second half of 2015. In order to support this, the method of measuring these numbers needed to be included in the "Method of Evaluation." In the case of Pet Community Center, the organization partnered with the Metro- Nashville government to obtain statistics for previous months and the current number of intakes. This is just one method, and the generally-accepted idea is there should be three methods of evaluation. Different time frames of gathering information should also be planned, from once a month to quarterly, bi-annually, or annually. The more information gathered here, the better; this section is how the grant reviewers will be able to track the grant usage and ensure it continues to be used to the fullest potential.

The importance of adequate evaluation cannot be stressed enough. Evaluation will be used to identify the program's strengths and weaknesses and indicate where adjustments need to be made. Most grant writers accept the knowledge that proposals will be in need of adjustment at some point. Until a program is implemented, scenarios or changes will become visible. If the grant writer can include some anticipated areas of adjustment or plans for using the evaluation tools for changes, the organization will continue to gain the confidence of the reviewing committee.

A realistic yet flattering light is the most desirable way to present this information. While writing about an organization's weakness can seem self-defeating, being open and honest on a grant will have better results. An example of this could be one of the grant examples already mentioned. Let us suppose a school that applied for the $30,000 grant for schools in Metro-Nashville was already understaffed. This is a weakness— how would an already stretched staff accomplish more? This is the portion of the grant proposal is where you can address that issue.

The organization would need to be contacted for this information unless the writer actually works in the industry; otherwise, how could the writer know what was a realistic option for the school? The writer could state a contingency plan for this situation should the program outgrow the current capacity of employees of the school. When the reviewing committee sees the organization seeking the grant has already thought ahead for potential challenges, the element of transparency and assurance of proper funding utilization will be reinforced. Once this has been effectively conveyed, the writer is able to move on to the "Project Timeline."

Project Timeline

The majority of the "Project Timeline" information will be provided to a freelance writer, as the writer will not be familiar enough with the organization to complete this section. This section can also be called "Process Objectives" in some instances (Galaskiewicz, et al, 1998, p.67). The timeline will paint a picture of implementation of the grant. This timeline will show the grant money flowing into the organization and back out into the community to achieve the goal. A program called Microsoft Project can be used to run some of the data and the plan, should the grant writer not have the information supplied. This section should be detailed enough to include staff hiring dates if additional staff are on-boarding for the project, program launch dates, and evaluation dates at the minimum. The more detail here, the better. This is the section where the planning for the use of the grant is really visible to the reviewing committee.

Some graphs and charts can be utilized in this section, especially if Microsoft Project is used, but putting them in an Appendix at the end of the proposal may be best. Otherwise, the graphs can distract from the actual plan and may appear to be placed to take up space and ensure the required numbers of pages are met. The bigger the project and grant, the longer this section will be; as this will vary dramatically for different grants, you do not need to keep in mind a minimum or maximum for generalizations. The key people responsible for the project need to be named in this section, and you should seek input to ensure the ability to complete the project. An organization member who has been working on the project for over a year would have a very good idea of how the timeline should play out and can be a wonderful resource for a grant writer.

One idea to keep in mind for this section, more so when the grant writer actually prepares it than when the organization provides the information, is if this plan is realistic. Can these tasks and projects be feasibly completed in the time frame provided? This is one reason having a Project Manager for larger grants is helpful; they are trained in planning large-scale undertakings and would be better equipped to analyze the timeline. The longer the grant and project, the harder this can be for a writer to complete. Some of the deadlines may actually be dictated by the grant itself, as some have very specific implementation or completion dates. If the project timeline does not maintain these dates, it will be very difficult for the proposal to be chosen for the grant award. Utilizing the sources and people within the organization in this section will be key. This section will really showcase how well the organization is planning for the grant, so being complete, concise, and detailed to ensure the reviewing committee can see the effort of planning is essential. The next section is titled "Credentials," and many of the people mentioned in "Project Timeline" will more than likely appear in this section as well.

Credentials

The "Credentials" section will vary in length depending on the size and scope of the organization and the specific grant. If the grant is small and only involves a small organization, the writer will have less information to relay. This section answers the basic question of why this organization should be considered qualified to undertake this project. How does this organization demonstrate the tools to succeed? In most cases, including the information on the Board of Directors, Officers, and any other key players in the project specifically will be applicable. Depending on the age and size of the organization, the information may be mostly referring to the individual's accomplishments both within and outside of the organization as well as their professional resumes in some capacity. In a larger organization with a large project this section can be longer, as needed. According to Hager, Rooney, and Pollack (2006), adequately explaining the credentials of the people who will be responsible for the grants funds to the proposal reviewers is critical (p. 313). This section is fairly straightforward and self-explanatory, and the information is easy to obtain from most organizations. This section is the last section in the Narrative, and leads into the Hook, Budget, and other sections.

A good rule of thumb is to answer a few questions within the Narrative, such as what organization wants. What specific need will the organization be addressing with the grant, and who will benefit from the program? The answers to these questions are usually preferable to place in the first section, to show the reviewing committee right away this organization should be a contender. Next, what objectives are being accomplished with the grant, and how will this be measured? As mentioned above, this is found in the "Method of Evaluation" section. An integral idea to convey is how the organization will use the grant in a way that aligns closely with the funding source. The closer this aligns, the more the funding source will understand the project and see it as a worthy endeavor. A grant proposal is almost a business plan; you would find these questions in a basic business plan, as well as when a business owner is requesting funding from an outside source. The last question— which is also important for you, the writer— is who is this organization requesting funding from? What do they stand for overall? The answer to this will assist in the tone of the proposal, as well as adding some heart in the writing.

The Hook

The Hook is the portion of the grant that tailors the idea of the organization to the funder of the grant. This is similar to an abstract for an academic paper. Many grant reviewers will read this first and decide if the rest of the proposal should be reviewed or if the organization does not align with what the funder wants. The goal is to quickly swing the review panel one way or the other, so the Hook is the sales pitch of the proposal. I recommend waiting to build this section until the end. Once all of the information is in place, writing a conclusive summary becomes much easier. This section may also be referred to as the Executive Summary and should be a page or less.

One element to keep in mind is that this is a summary. Do not introduce new elements or ideas in the summary. Many of the answers to questions asked in the beginning of research will be useful here—the identity of the organization, the mission and vision, and other organizational information. This section needs to answer what the program or service being proposed is and why it is needed in the community. Why is this project important, and what makes this organization the best choice for the grant?

All of these ideas and questions need to be addressed in the Hook, but they cannot just be stated and answered; there needs to be a pitch behind the words. The more interesting to read, the more the reviewers will be inclined to investigate the rest of the proposal. If the Hook is dryly written and not engaging, the rest of the proposal may not appear to be appealing to the review committee. For writers who do not see themselves as strong in persuasive writing, this section can be a challenging, but again, it is easier to complete after the rest of the proposal is finished.

The Budget

The Budget is a large section, but this information will typically be provided by the organizations seeking the grant for the writer to organize into a logical manner. This section is occasionally placed in "Project Timeline." The timeline for completion is based on funding most of the time, so these two sections may have some repeat information but are necessary to include in order to answer all of the review committee's possible questions (Dees, et al., 2002, p. 100). A few topics will normally be addressed in this section, such as cost projections, cost assessments, and graphs and charts. The question of whether the budget is realistic must be addressed. Evidence of the plan could be bids from contractors, teacher's salaries, or any number of things to help show that this cost was not pulled out of thin air. Details are good here, and this section can sometimes be the largest of the proposal depending on the depth of the grant.

Occasionally, the funding source will place limitations on the grant or request specific information in the proposal. Some organizations require a specific budget form. Writers must be sure to investigate the requirements thoroughly. In most cases, the budget information will be provided by the organization seeking the grant, and you may not change or alter these numbers in anyway (Beaufort, 1999, p.45).

Access to the records may be allowed and some budgetary calls may be left to your discretion, especially when you are employed by one organization alone. Having the final budget signed off by someone in the organization is recommended, either someone with finance involvement or directly involved with the project. Charts and graphs are great ways to illustrate the budget, but only use what is needed so the proposal is not cluttered and the figures do not seem to act as fillers. The Budget section is typically straightforward and easy to construct.

The Appendix

The last section usually contains supporting materials for various points throughout the proposal. Typically called an Appendix , this section can include certifications, charts, tables, graphs, and other visual aids. Before building the Appendix, double check the grant guidelines, as some funders have specific requirements and restrictions on this section. This can be a time-consuming section, dealing with tables and graphics, but will add spunk to the proposal. Many writers are left-brained, so the amount of numbers involved in this section can be overwhelming. Remember that you do not actually need to compute the data; it helps.If you are a creative person, this can be the most fun section to design. The Appendix has no set length since there different grants will have different needs. The longer the program or the larger the organization, the longer this section may be.

Authorized Signatures

Once the Appendix is complete and the proposal has been put together, edited, and reviewed, it is time for the authorized signatures. Most grants will require a signature from someone in a leadership position at the organization— these signatures are typically from CEOs, CFOs, and Presidents, so there may be some lag time between returning the proposal to them and their ability to review and sign it. Make sure you do not wait until close to the deadline for this portion. At times, circumstances result in having the proposal ready uncomfortably close to the deadline, but you should do your best to avoid this out of respect to the leaders of the organization and professionalism. Different grants will require different signatures, so review the requirements well and identify who the corresponding people in the organization are early on in the process. There may be some edits to make once the grant is reviewed by these persons, such as detail changes or requests to add or remove information or rework a section.

Formatting and Concluding the Proposal

Some basic specifications can be expected with a grant proposal, but it is very important to double check before formatting. One of the key specifications is how many pages are allowed or required, which can greatly impact the writing approach and can sometimes help decide what to include in the proposal. Writers should verify what formatting style is required for the proposal. Most grants are accepted in APA format, but there have been a few that preferred MLA. In 2016, all grants needed to be typed in a word processing program, and some review committees wanted single spaced while others required double. This can be a game changer if the requirement is 10 pages typed double spaced but a writer typed single spaced— nearly half of the information included would be over the page limit, so the whole grant proposal would need to be reworked. Knowing the format requirements before beginning can save time for the writer and the organization. Some grants will request cover pages while others consider them optional. All of this should be laid out in the grant information, and if not, the writers can go back to the initial contact and try and find the answers through the funding source. This is usually much less time consuming than guessing or assuming.

I have learned a few tricks and tips through my own experience. I always have a proposal reviewed by a colleague as well as someone outside the business. This ensures that both people who understand the grant and those new to the industry can follow the proposal; you cannot know how well-versed the grant review committee will be, so this ensures the proposal is clear. A fine line exists between assuming knowledge of the reader and overelaborating an idea. By having someone who has limited knowledge about the proposal review it, you assure that knowledge is not being assumed. When the colleague within the industry reviews it, they will be able to tell if there is too much information. The best idea is to meet somewhere in the middle for the highest quality and a well-received proposal.

Please make sure your proposal is neat, organized, and on time. Being on time can mean the difference between being consideration and dismissal. As a follow up, I suggest contacting the person in the funding organization again. There is nothing wrong with inquiring about the status and outcome of the grant; this keeps your organization's name in the fore front. I compare this to following up after a job interview: it can make a memorable impression and alleviate some worry on the grant writer's part; the waiting game can seem eternal at times.

References

Beaufort, A. (1999). *Writing in the real world: Making the transition from school to work*. Boston, MA: Teachers College Press.

Bray, I. (2013). *Effective fundraising for non-profits: Real-world strategies that work*. (4th ed). Berkley, CA: NOLO.

Dees, G. J., Emerson, J., & Economy, P.(2002). *Enterprising non-profits: A toolkit for social entrepreneurs*. New York, NY: John Wiley & Sons.

Galaskiewicz, J. & Bielefeld, W. (1998). *Nonprofit organizations in an age of uncertainty*. Hawthorne, NY: Aldine De Gruyter.

Hager, M., Rooney, P., & Pollack, T. (2006). How fundraising is carried out in US nonprofit organization. *International Journal of Non-Profit and Voluntary Sector Marketing*, 7(4), 311-324.

Hall, M. S., & Howlett, S. (2003). *Getting funded: The complete guide to writing grant proposals*.(4th ed.) Portland, OR: Portland State University.

Karsh, E., & Fox, A. S. (2014). *The only grant writing book you'll ever need*. (4th ed). New York, NY: Basic Books.

Thompson, W. (2003). *The complete idiot's guide to grant writing*. New York, NY: Alpha Group.

Wason, S. (2004). *Webster's new world grant writing handbook*. Hoboken, NJ: Wiley, Inc.

Young, D. (Ed.). (2007). *Financing nonprofits: putting theory into practice*. Lanham, MD: AltaMira Press.

Writing Resumes and Cover Letters for Success
Bonnie Flynn

The first recorded professional résumé was prepared by Leonardo Da Vinci in 1482. At the age of 30, he sent a handwritten letter with a list of his capabilities to Lovecio il Moro, Duke of Milan (Cenedella, n.d.). Part of it says, as translated from Italian, "I have kinds of mortars, most convenient and easy to carry, and with these I can fling small stones almost resembling a storm" (para. 9). His words were descriptive and persuasive, emphasizing what he could do, based on the needs of the Duke. In many respects, the modern résumé is not much different than Da Vinci's, at least in regards to what he wanted to accomplish – get a job!

The résumé has evolved over the years, becoming a professional marketing tool enabling the eager job seeker to put his best foot forward and knock the socks off the next potential employer. The résumé provides a brief summary of a person's experience, education, and skills designed to interest a potential employer (Crosby, 2009).

Writing a résumé in the digital age is much easier than it was in the past. Word processing programs have built-in template guides for preparing a résumé. The Internet has tons of completed résumé examples to use as a starting point. Organizations are available to review your résumé, often for a fee. In addition, the application process is automated, allowing for ease of submission. There is no need to buy reams of expensive parchment paper, purchase rolls of postage stamps or make a special trip to the post office to mail that beautifully crafted résumé and cover letter. An applicant can upload the résumé and send it into cyber space to be reviewed by the eager recruiter on the receiving end. However, while the process has been somewhat simplified, it now faces new challenges.

While you are sending off your résumé with the click of a button, so are hundreds— maybe even thousands— of others. You have no idea if it was actually received by the potential employer unless you get an automated response acknowledging your submission. You have no idea what format that carefully constructed résumé was delivered in once downloaded by the receiving party or if your résumé will be read and accepted or rejected by a real person or a machine.

Preparing a résumé can be a daunting task, but being focused in your approach can make the process easier. Four basic steps in creating a résumé are as follows: compiling information about yourself and the occupations that interest you, choosing a format, adding personal style, and, last but not least, proofreading the document before it becomes final (Crosby, 2009).

The accompanying cover letter is just as important as the résumé (Sweeney, n.d.). A cover letter is an introduction to your résumé that sparks an employer's interest in you and, if done well, creates an impression of competence (Crosby, 2009; LiveCareer, n.d.).

According to Sweeney (n.d.), the cover letter should accomplish the following objectives:
1) Give the potential employer a reason to be interested in you. Accomplish this by highlighting the most relevant skills and experience from your résumé with details explaining how these qualifications make you the best candidate for the job.
2) Explain why you are interested in the job and the company. Show your enthusiasm for the position and

highlight your awareness of the job by doing your research ahead of time.

3) Lay the groundwork for future contact and set yourself up for an interview. Let the potential employer know when you will follow up with them or how they can reach you.

There are some rules of thumb when preparing a résumé and cover letter. It is both an art and a science, but you do not need to be Leonardo Da Vinci (who supposedly thought of himself as both an artist and a scientist) to prepare the perfect résumé and cover letter. According to Morton (2015), "Good résumé form won't guarantee a homerun, but bad résumé form can take you out of the game" (p. 1).

Below are ten things to consider when designing your résumé and cover letter.

10. Get organized and stay organized.

According to Crosby (2009), a résumé is a brief summary of a person's education, experience, and skills. Most résumés contain the following components: contact information, qualifications summary, education, experience, activities and associations, special skills, awards and honors, and other personal information.

The most popular format is the chronological, but, depending upon your needs, you may want to consider a functional type of résumé or even a combination of both chronological and functional formats. According to Simply Hired (2013), the chronological résumé begins by listing work history, starting with the most recent position and continuing in reverse chronological order. Key accomplishments and qualifications give potential employers a sense of the kind of work you have done and what you are capable of doing. An education section follows, including the school(s) attended and when, degree(s) earned, and any honors/awards received. New graduates should list education first and then experience. More seasoned professionals should list experience before education. At the end, include a skills section to highlight such things as computer skills, laboratory skills, and any languages spoken. This type of résumé benefits job seekers with a strong work history.

Another type is the functional résumé. This option may be preferred for those who have a scanty work history with gaps in employment or for career changers. According to Crosby (2009), to create a functional résumé, first identify three or four skills necessary for your target job. For each of those skills, identify three to five concrete examples which demonstrate that ability, using action phrases when writing the list. The skills should be arranged in order of importance. The last section of the functional résumé should be a brief work history, noting job titles, company names, and years of employment. Any gaps in work history can be explained in the cover letter.

The combination résumé merges elements of both the chronological and functional. These résumés are varied based on the histories they summarize. One variation starts with a chronological format but then subdivides each job description into skill categories. Another type of combination résumé utilizes a functional format listing examples of the skills, but then identifies the organization where each example occurred (Crosby, 2009).

While the chronological is the most popular, and preferred, résumé format, do not be afraid to choose another style if it better fits your situation.

9. The résumé should be the perfect balance between succinct and detailed.

Lengthy résumés can be cumbersome for recruiters and hiring managers to read. Résumés that are too short may not tell the whole story. A good rule of thumb is to aim for a two-page résumé. A two-page résumé seems to be long enough to contain sufficient detail but not too long to be onerous to review. Do not make the font too small. The hiring manager should not need a magnifying glass to read the résumé or cover letter! Stick to more traditional fonts, such as Ariel, Times New Roman, or Courier.

Since most résumés these days are emailed or uploaded electronically rather than mailed through the postal service, you do not need to invest in reams of expensive résumé paper. However, bringing a copy of the résumé to an interview is a good idea, so you may find it worth investing in a package of higher-quality paper for those occasions. Sometimes, résumés are cut-and-pasted onto an online application form, and the formatting may be thrown off. While that is unavoidable, you should still take care when preparing the résumé. It should be pleasing to the eye and readable.

According to Enelow and Kursmark (2016), you should keep your writing tight, clear, and concise. Do not include irrelevant experience or unnecessary details. More than one review may be needed to figure out what is important to include and what should be eliminated. Konop (2014) claims that the average résumé gets approximately six seconds of review before it is either retained or pitched, so make those words count!

According to Barraclough (2012), job seekers should qualify and quantify their important achievements. If you held a sales position and were the top salesperson in the region, back it up with a number; for example, "Achieved top sales for the Midwest region averaging $1 million in yearly revenue." This statement not only gives a specific amount but also sets the stage and provides an opportunity for dialogue during the interview process.

Some "don'ts" to consider when preparing a résumé:
Don't include references with the résumé. It is usually sufficient to note "References submitted upon request" at the bottom of the résumé. However, if the prospective job requires references at

the time of application, make sure to get permission from the people before including their contact information. Getting permission ahead of time is a matter of courtesy and, in the lucky event they are contacted, ensures they will not be blindsided and will be prepared with an appropriate response. You could either include the requested list of references on a separate piece of paper or within the cover letter, unless otherwise instructed.

Don't include information related to salary in the résumé or cover letter, unless, again, required to do so when submitting the application. Then, it becomes your choice. There are differing opinions on this. Some experts feel that you should *never* include salary information, no matter what. However, in that case, you are taking a chance. If it means that the application will be tossed in the circular file, it may be worth including the information. Salary information could be included in the cover letter if you choose to provide it.

8. Watch the buzzwords, but key in on keywords.
Resist the urge to sound too "cool." Generally, experienced hiring managers are sophisticated enough to know the difference between trite and sincere. Words like "proactive," "motivated," and "enthusiastic" are buzzwords job seekers associate with a well-written cover letter and résumé. But when those words become overused, they become platitudes and clichés to avoid (Casserly, 2011). If you decide to use a buzzword, list specific examples of how it describes you. If you say you are a team player, what experience do you have working on a team? What were your contributions to the success of the team?

While buzzwords should be kept to a minimum, it is important to note that recruiters often use software that spots certain keywords on résumés and cover letters. Look for common keywords specific to your occupation of interest, such as in job advertisements or job descriptions, and find opportunities to strategically insert those words throughout both the résumé and cover letter. Of course, if those words refer to particular skill or competency, make sure to be able to substantiate your claim—which leads to the next point:

7. Tell the truth.

Nothing is worse than being caught with your proverbial pants down during an interview or, worse yet, getting hired for a job based on something noted on a résumé or cover letter that is simply not true. Benjamin Franklin did not say "honesty is the best policy" just because it was a cute-sounding idiom. We all want to put our best foot forward when job hunting, but it is better to be hired for what you *actually* can do rather than what you want people to *think* you can do. Do not say you have a degree or certificate in something unless you really have it. If you are working on completing a degree and have an end date, note that on the résumé—"anticipated graduation (date)." Otherwise, these seemingly small lies can have disastrous consequences, and you may have to do some serious back-pedaling.

6. Use action verbs.

Ah, those magical action verbs: words such as "advised," processed," "developed," "created," and "sold" can paint a picture of your background, experience, education, and accomplishments. Of course, as noted above, the chosen words should be accurate, and you should be prepared to cite concrete examples in case you are asked during an interview.

According to Walraven (2012), keep verbs in the present tense for current jobs and in the past tense for previous jobs. Make sure the verb tenses are consistent within each heading, with one exception: for current jobs, if describing something you *used to do*, it is acceptable to use the past tense. In other words, if you "developed a system to process expense reports in an expeditious manner, saving the company $1000 per quarter in late fees," it would be appropriate to list that in the past tense.

5. Use the cover letter to introduce yourself.
Whether or not to include a cover letter when submitting a résumé has been the subject of recent controversy. If applying for a job which specifically tells you *not* to include a cover letter, then it may be best to not include it. Otherwise, including a cover letter is good form. The cover letter is a way of introducing yourself to the potential employer. Developing a standard template to use as a basis for the cover letter is acceptable, but each letter should be customized for the specific job to which you are applying.

The cover letter should complement and highlight points in the résumé and should be limited to one page. It should have a natural flow—with a beginning, middle, and end (Fisher, n.d.). According to Marshall Brown and Associates (2013), each paragraph in the cover letter has a purpose— specifically, "the hook, the pitch and the close." The beginning paragraph should state the position to which you are applying and introduce your qualifications. The second paragraph is the "meat and potatoes" of the cover letter, stating what you can bring to the position. Here, you can explain gaps in employment, but you should not dwell on weaknesses (Barraclough, 2012). Use this opportunity to sell yourself and highlight specific skills that the job is requesting, even if noted in the résumé. Use specific language from the job advertisement to make the language appropriate to the position. Use positive rather than hesitant language, such as "I am confident I can" rather than "I believe that I can" (Fisher, n.d.). The closing paragraph briefly wraps up the letter, offering one last reason why you should be considered for the position, thanking the reader for his or her time, and stating preferred contact information.

The overall tone of the cover letter should be positive, confident, and inviting. The cover letter should not be boring, but be interesting and readable. Make sure it relates to information that the potential employer cares about. Show that you read the job advertisement and/or description and put some real thought into your cover letter (LiveCareer, n.d.). This will put you one step closer to getting that dream job.

4. Share what makes you special.

While résumés and cover letters should sound professional, be truthful, avoid buzzwords, and be the perfect balance between succinct and detailed, and share what makes you special. Briefly include such things as professional credentials, professional affiliations, board of director appointments and other leadership positions, public speaking engagements, and publications (Enelow & Kursmark, 2016). Résumé reading can get pretty boring. What makes your résumé stand out from those in the rest of the pile? Why would a hiring manager want to consider you for a job? What is that *je ne sais quoi* or special something that only *you* possess?

3. Certain job search situations call for more than one résumé.

Modify your résumé for different industries (Infinity Staffing, 2016). Compile different résumés emphasizing competencies and experiences particular to other skillsets you may possess if you are planning to explore different types of jobs in your search. For instance, you may have one résumé for a job in education and another for a sales job if those are your areas of interest.

Different industries require various credentials and skills. Some occupations may want a formal résumé while others call for it to be creative (Infinity Staffing, 2016). Do not be boxed in to a one-size-fits-all document, especially if you plan to expand your horizons and are open to various job opportunities.

2. Think of the résumé as a living document.

Always have an updated résumé stored and accessible, ready to go. You never know when the opportunity to apply for that perfect job will land in your lap. You may want to apply for graduate school and need to submit a résumé. Your current company could offer a new position that would be a wise career move. Conversely— and this is the worst-case scenario—, you never know if you will suddenly find yourself out of a job. It is better to be proactive and prepared for that moment than to be scrambling to compose the perfect résumé and cover letter.

Review, update, and revise your résumé frequently. As soon as you complete a degree or certificate or receive an award, note it on your résumé. If you change jobs or positions within your current company, or even if duties change in your present appointment, update that information right away to keep your résumé fresh and as current as possible.

1. Last, but not least: proofread, proofread, proofread!
Your résumé is beautifully crafted with eloquent phrases listing all your wonderful accomplishments, but why are you not receiving calls? Perhaps it is something as simple as "Pays attention to *detials*" noted on the bottom of page two.

It is easy to miss seemingly simple errors after working closely on a document. However, overlooked errors can be seen as glaring missteps to another person. Grammar and spellchecking software should be run every time you make changes to the copy. They may not catch every error, but they should catch some of the more obvious ones. However, do not stop there. Read over the draft one more time. Then, put the résumé and cover letter aside for an hour, a day, or a week, and read it again with fresh eyes. Read it out loud to yourself or have someone else read it out loud to you. You would be amazed what the ears pick up that the eyes do not. Have your mother read your résumé. Have your spouse read your résumé. Have your children read your résumé. Even ask the next door neighbor to read your résumé. It is better to have a family member or friend find an error than a potential employer. Besides just finding errors, the reader may offer suggestions for enhancement that you overlooked. You do not have to take the suggestion, but it does not hurt to consider it.

Your résumé may not be around as long as Da Vinci's, but who knows? As Will Rogers said, "you never get a second chance to make a first impression." This is your story. Make it a good one that will ensure that you stand out from the rest.

References

Barraclough, E. (2012). How to land a job in a tough climate. *Managing Intellectual Property*. (219), 101.

Casserly, M. (2011). Ten clichés to ditch on the job hunt. *Forbes.com*. Retrieved from http://www.forbes.com/sites/meghancasserly/2011/09/15/ten-cliches-to-ditch-on-the-job-hunt/#49cd1e414839

Cenedella, M. (n.d.). Even a genius has to sell himself...The resume of leonardo da vinci [Web log post]. Retrieved from https://www.theladders.com/career-advice/leonardo-da-vincis-resume/

Crosby, O. (2009). Résumés, applications and cover letters. *Occupational Outlook Quarterly*. *53*(2), 18-29.

Enelow, W. & Kursmark, L. (2016). Writing powerful, impactful and memorable HR resumes. *Society for Human Resource Management*. Retrieved from https://www.shrm.org/hrdisciplines/orgempdev/articles/pages/how-to-create-an-hr-resume.aspx

Fisher, P. (n.d.). 6 essentials of great cover letter writing. Retrieved from http://ewjobready.org/6-essentails-of-great-cover-letter-writing.html

Infinity Staffing. (2016). The dos and don'ts of writing a resume [Web log post]. Retrieved from http://infinity–staffing.biz/blog/writing-a-resume/

Konop, J. (2014). The 5 essential elements your resume needs. *Forbes.com*. Retrieved from http://www.forbes.com/sites/nextavenue/2014/05/19/the-5-essential-elements-your-resume-needs/#32189fd65d80

LiveCareer. (n.d.). How a great cover letter can change your job search. Retrieved from https://www.livecareer.com/cover-letter-tips

Marshall Brown & Associates. (2013). Writing a successful cover letter. Retrieved from http://jobs.pedjobs.org/pics/gui/clc/cover_letter.pdf

Morton, R. (2016). How to write a winning resume. *American College of Healthcare Executives.* Retrieved from https://www.ache.org/newclub/career/GUIDES/RESUME.cfm

Simply Hired. (2013). The 3 main types of resumes [Web log post]. Retrieved from http://www.simplyhired.com/blog/jobsearch/resumes/3-main-types-resumes/

Sweeney, L. (n.d.). Cover letter basics. Retrieved from https://www.experience.com/alumnus/article?channel_id=Resumes&source_page=additional_articles&article_id=article_1126286326107

Walraven, J. (2016). When to use past or present tense in a resume? *Design Resumes.* Retrieved from http://designresumes.com/2012/05/top-resume-question-when-to-use-past-tense-or-present-tense/

Special Topics

Community Education:
Bridging the Gap to Creative Thinking
Oluwakemi Elufiede and
Carissa Barker-Stucky

Introduction

The purpose of this chapter is to provide a framework for facilitating creative writing workshops in the community. This framework was created by Oluwakemi Elufiede, Founder and President of Carnegie Writers, Inc. Currently, the framework is utilized by interns and volunteers who facilitate teen and adult creative writing workshops. In 2015, Oluwakemi Elufiede and Carissa Barker-Stucky developed the manual for writing facilitators, entitled *Community Education: Bridging the Gap to Creative Thinking*. This manual is used to train interns and volunteers. The components of this chapter include the following: the facilitator role, creative thinking, community education, learning styles, workshop structure and activities, workshop planning, and writing for publication.

Facilitator Role

Understanding the role of a facilitator is the key component to being effective in an author workshop. As a facilitator, you will act as guides for aspiring writers, coaches. You are not there to command but to instruct and lead. The below lists highlight areas facilitators should be comfortable with and characteristics of a quality workshop leader. (Gospe, 2016)

Facilitator Competencies:
- Intentional use of time and space;
- Talent in encouraging participation and creativity;

- Affirms the group's good decisions/practices;
- Remains objective and subjective;
- Reads and understands the underlying dynamics of the group;
- Assumes responsibility for the group's improvement and practice;
- Properly documents group's journey and provides resources;
- Acts in a professional, confident, and authentic manner; and
- Maintains personal integrity.

Characteristics of the Facilitator:
- "Asking" rather than "telling";
- Spending time building relationships rather than always being task-oriented;
- Listening without interrupting;
- More enthusiastic than systematic; and
- More like a coach than a scientist.

The above characteristics are vital in leading an effective workshop. Asking questions rather than simply telling a participant what to do helps guide the writer's creative process. Spending time building relationships can help you learn the writers' various quirks; this allows for better identification of learning styles in addition to writing styles—perhaps someone turning in a bit of fiction has a flare for poetry, etc. Being more enthusiastic helps to encourage the writers rather than making the workshop feel like another stifling classroom.

Creative Thinking

The process for creative thinking must include flexibility, originality, fluency, and elaboration. With these steps, people are able to recognize, imagine, initiate, collaborate, assess, evaluate, and celebrate their unique ideas. While there is no real formula for the creative process, certain stages have been discussed by writers of all ages. No one approach works for all writers, but knowing the various stages can help a writer learn how to approach their projects in a way that will suit them.

Recognize
The first stage in the creative process is finding a project. Writers can be prompted by peers or teachers, find a contest to enter, notice a niche to be filled, or discover a story waiting to be told. Writers should learn to recognize the various opportunities they are presented with and expand them into a project. Learning to recognize challenges and opportunities helps maintain a healthy mind. This recognition is not limited to fictional work: journalists recognize a story to present; scientists recognize an experiment to be researched and shared; etc.

Imagine
For some, the easiest stage; for others, the most difficult—now that a project has been recognized, the writers must develop unique ideas to form their story, poem, or article. Writers must learn how to think flexibly, using both divergent and convergent processes. Different things can inspire the imagination of different writers. Some think better in silence, others prefer music or a hot cup of coffee. Helping writers learn to stimulate their imagination can be as simple as providing prompts, but not everyone has immediate access to their treasure trove of ideas. Experimenting with different brainstorming activities can help writers learn to follow their creative paths when plotting their projects.

Initiate and Collaborate
Now that the writer has a project and an idea of what to do with it, it is time to sit down and get to work. Some writers work well on their own while others prefer to talk out ideas with peers. Taking time to read projects out or brainstorm with a partner can help open ideas for the writer. The collaboration stage is an important step for facilitators: this is where you practice interpersonal and leadership skills, helping your writers through

the various stages of their projects and working with them to achieve their goals.

Assess

This stage intertwines with the others. It involves taking a step back from the project and giving it an objective look. Is the project working out? Is something wrong? Did something change that still works? Are you meeting your deadlines? Peer review is a wonderful tool in the assessment stage, as the writer is often too close to the project to look at it objectively. Sometimes assessment leads to revision, other times it leads to scrapping a project and trying again or trying something else. Writers should not feel discouraged when something does not work out; instead, encourage them to take note of what changed and use the information for later projects.

Evaluate & Celebrate

Perhaps the most important stage; writers need to remember to look back on the process and celebrate their project's completion. Encourage writers to take notes of what helped their process and what stunted it. Celebrate successful team projects and assistance, and keep a list of any writing resources introduced during workshops for later reference. Though rejection and scrapped projects are part of the process, celebrating successes can alleviate many of the perceived failures.

Community Education

A Facilitator provides a form of community service through education. Community education embraces the educational belief for lifelong learning process. Community education occurs through special interest groups, hobbies, friendships, associations, and religious affiliations. According to Nashville Community Education (2016), community education provides personal and professional enrichment that impacts exploration and community networking. People feel connected to others through community-based activities that, in return, cater to lifelong learning.

For facilitators, they are teaching teens and adults. Both groups include a variety of personalities, experiences, and learning styles. Pappas (2013) noted that adults are considered mature, confident, practical, effective, decision makers, and self-directed. In comparison to children, adults have a self-concept that is a more independent and the self-directed approach for the accumulation of life experience (Beder and Merriam, 1982). However, children also provide a value to the learning environment based on their learning experiences in school and in their daily living activities. Learners want to be valued for their unique characteristics and respected for their differences.

Therefore, you as a facilitator must understand pedagogy vs. andragogy. Knowles (1980) explains the difference between pedagogy and andragogy in relation to role of learners' experience, readiness to learn, and orientation to learning. With pedagogy, the role of learner experiences provides little benefit to the learning situation. People are ready to learn; learners see education as a process of acquiring subject-matter content. With andragogy, as people grow, they accumulate experiences that become increasingly rich in response to their learning experiences. People become ready to learn something when they need to learn in relation to their competence toward a fulfilling lifestyle.

Learning Styles

Potential writers do not fit a single mold. In fact, there are eight molds for a facilitator to consider—the eight learning styles. These styles are Verbal, Visual, Musical/Auditory, Physical/Kinesthetic, Logical/Mathematical, Social, Solitary, and Combination as shown in Figure 9.1.

Figure 9.1 Learning Styles

Verbal learners prefer to use words in both speech and writing. The best way to help a Verbal through a workshop is to talk to them. Brainstorm out loud or explain a concept to guide their work.

Visual learners respond well to images or pictures, graphs or charts. Handouts are helpful to these students—any form of visual reference. A good exercise for visual learners is to take a selection of inkblots, have them pick out three objects they see, and then have the participants write a piece based on those perceived objects.

Auditory learners absorb information best through sound, including music. These types of students respond well to background music or may choose to wear headphones while writing. Rhythm mnemonics are especially helpful in teaching key concepts.

Kinesthetic learners, or Physical learners, like to use their hands or body to learn concepts. Exercises that require acting out ideas or describing facial expressions can help bolster their writing.

Logical learners, or Mathematical learners, appreciate systems and sequences. They learn easier when they can use logic to reason something out. To help the logically and mathematically minded, present the act of writing as a puzzle to solve. A possible exercise is to provide a scenario and have the writer come up with a solution.

Social learners work best in group environments. A plethora of activities exist for small group writing, including progressive stories and peer edit sessions. Mixing groups between activities also introduces learners to new influences.

Solitary learners do best working on their own. They may come together as a group to share results from a writing prompt, but they do the work alone. Facilitators should prepare writing prompts to pass around but should not insist that all writers pair up. Let the participant do what is most comfortable for them.

Facilitators should be aware that not all writers will fall into one category or another. Many aspiring learners benefit from a combination of styles. Use exercises and discussion to work out which styles work best for which writers. Encourage learners who are struggling by pointing out that they will benefit from figuring out which style or styles fit them best.

Workshop Content, Activities, and Structure

In preparation for the workshop, determine workshop content, plan writing activities, and develop a consistent structure. Workshop content is based on what you plan to discuss during the workshop as it relates to writing genres. The content should be discussed with co-facilitators, if applicable. Writing activities are integral to consistent engagement from the learner as the facilitator should not dominate the learning environment with only their ideas, but be open to encourage the learners to utilize their critical thinking skills. The workshop should include power writing, progressive story writing, writing prompts, and a writers workshop.

Power writing is a timed free-writing exercise that may or may not include a one-word prompt. This is a warm-up activity completed at the beginning of each class. A progressive story is a collaborative writing activity that includes several individuals providing a contribution to the continuation of a story. Writing prompts can help writers with writer's block stimulate new ideas. A writers workshop is a peer review session that improves critical reading and writing skills. The writer is able to receive feedback from the reader for the development of the writer-reader relationship. With these activities, writers are able to explore, analyze and brainstorm new writing techniques, which impact their writing skills.

Figure 9.2 Workshop Elements

Workshop Planning

Planning a workshop relies heavily on three core considerations: what you want students to learn, what activities you will use, and how you will check for understanding. For the beginning facilitator, a good model to follow is shown in Figure 8.2. Experienced facilitators will be more comfortable in leading workshops and may choose to break away from the pattern based on what they know of the upcoming event or the participating students.

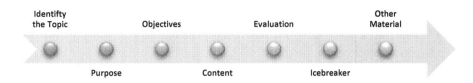

Figure 9.3 Workshop Planning

Identify the Topic
As shown in Figure 8.2, the first thing to consider is the topic. Facilitators must consider what type of workshop they are leading—what style of writing will the workshop cover? One, a combination, or all different types based on participant preference? Each type of writing has specific needs, and you as a Facilitator should be moderately comfortable with whatever style the workshop will cover.

Poetry
Poetry uses aesthetics and rhythms to evoke emotions within a reader. Some poems tell stories while others describe a feeling or a setting. Styles of poems vary, and as such you will want to spend more time on content and word choice than form. If a writer aims for a specific style—such as a Shakespearean/Elizabethan sonnet versus a Petrarchan sonnet, or aiming for the haiku style—then you have an opening to discuss form and meter. Grammar and punctuation also takes a back seat when discussing poetry, as there is more stylistic leeway.

Short Story
A short story can be either fiction or nonfiction. Short stories are shorter than novels, with the aim to be readable in one sitting. Most short stories are based on a single theme and focus on mood and characterization. The key components to a short story are as follows: Setting, Mood, Characters, Action/Problem, and Point of View. While most short stories follow the basic plot

outline of exposition, inciting action, rising action, climax, falling action, and denouement (otherwise known as the Freytag Model), some writers may take stylistic liberty by omitting certain stages. So long as the desired effect of the story remains, these stylistic liberties are encouraged.

Article Writing
Articles take a journalistic approach to inform and engage a reader through high-quality professional writing. Articles should aim to answer the Ws of journalism: who, what, when, where, and why. The first stage in writing an article is research—hearsay is not a source for good articles. Information should be checked, double checked, and triple checked whenever possible. Articles may also be accompanied by tasteful pictures, useful images, and/or diagrams. Whenever images are present, writers should ensure that their placement enhances the article rather than pulling the reader out. A key component to a good article, like any quality writing, is an eye-catching opening line—questions and interesting facts are common choices. Articles should always be written in the third person with an objective viewpoint. While active verbs are encouraged, some writers may prefer a more passive voice to keep the focus on their subject.

Flash Fiction
Flash fiction—also known as micro fiction, nano-fiction, quick fiction, and short short stories—is a complex style of writing with a variety of definitions. The basic component is length—flash fiction stories range from 1,500 words down; popular examples on the Internet can be as short as a single sentence. Writing flash fiction is an exercise in packing a lot of emotion into a small space; authors must learn how to eliminate unnecessary words and combine phrases in meaningful ways. While this style is difficult, it can also be very rewarding.

Novel Writing

Some authors attend workshops in order to assist their novel process. Depending on the length of the workshop, facilitators should decide ahead of time if an entire novel can be addressed or if the focus must be on a single chapter. Some authors may simply want feedback on a single concept, general plot, or character creation.

Lyric Writing/Songwriting

Lyric writing has a lot in common with poetry, especially regarding the use of rhythm and stylistic liberty. Lyric writers aim to put words to a song; songwriters aim to compose the music as well. The focus for lyric writers is the theme behind the song and the rhythmic qualities of their word choice.

Playwriting

Playwriting is the act of creating a script for an individual or group to perform in front of an audience. This style of writing focuses heavily on dialogue, keeping setting and direction to a minimum to allow performers creative liberty. Plays range in style from the number of acts and scenes to the number of characters.

Essay Writing

From academic to personal, essays permeate our lives. Essays focus heavily on structure and logic flow; some require sources with proper citation. Authors should start with the type of essay; you can then guide them through the brainstorm, outline, and/or research processes. Grammar is a key component in essays and thus should be a heavy focus during workshops.

Purpose and Objectives

The planning stages of Purpose and Objectives are tied together. Why is the workshop taking place? This question guides what type of activities you will use to encourage participants. For instance, an essay workshop may focus on grammar or structure while a short story workshop may focus on character creation or theme.

General workshops allow various purposes for each student and often require an icebreaker session for you to determine what approach will work best for each participant. The objectives of a workshop are the steps a facilitator uses to fulfill the purpose; for longer workshops, each session can fulfill an objective, and the objectives stack to reach the purpose. For shorter workshops, individual activities create the stepping stones. Objectives vary based on topic, but some common areas are discussed below.

Capturing a Unique Character Voice
The world is full of individuals; each person has their own sense of style, way of speaking, and other unique quirks. Some rely on colloquialisms when speaking or speak English as a second language and have a habit of using incorrect sentence structure. When it comes to dialogue, authors should consider how their character would speak in real life. Sentence fragments, poor grammar, etc. will often show up in conversations. Some authors may go as far as writing conversation phonetically in order to convey a thick accent or way of speaking—just be sure the reader can understand this character without massive amounts of frustration.

Dynamic Dialogue
Concepts to consider with dialogue are the objective, tactic, and obstacles. Why is the character driven to speak and interact? What do characters need to accomplish to attain their goal? What is preventing them? Does the character succeed, or do the obstacles prevail? These focuses help prevent dialogue from wandering and pulling away from the story.

Plot Structure
When it comes to fiction and playwriting, many authors wish to hone their skill with plot structures. As aforementioned, the most popular structure is the Freytag model. This model lays out the key components of a plot: exposition should introduce characters and settings; the inciting incident starts the action; rising action

builds momentum in the plot by introducing conflicts and developing character relationships; the climax is a turning point in the story, the peak of action or conflict; falling action occurs to wind down the story; and, finally, denouement occurs when all arcs in the plot have been resolved and questions answered. The type of writing determines how the structure should be maintained. A novel or book series, for instance, will have multiple plots tied into the overall story, whereas flash fiction may pick rising action and omit all other items.

Sentence Variety
An author's success relies heavily on their reader. No matter the type of writing, authors must keep their audience engaged. One of the easiest ways to lose an audience is monotonous sentence structure. Switching between long and short, complex and simple, and fragments or full sentences helps add rhythm to the words and carry a reader along. When people speak, they vary their word structure instinctively; authors should seek that same variety.

Flow
Another way to lose a reader is abrupt shifts. If an author is talking about dogs in one paragraph and then suddenly starts describing their car, a reader will be pulled out of the work as they attempt to process the shift. In an essay, points should flow together to build towards a single conclusion that fulfills the beginning thesis—if an author is writing an argumentative essay about whether dogs or cats make better pets, they should not start discussing goldfish. Some stories make use of abrupt shifts between characters, but authors must be careful to include hints that allow their readers to understand the shift. Breaks in the text can help convey a change, as can a chapter shift and careful choice of words in the first few sentences.

Content and Evaluation

Once the topic, purpose, and objectives are determined, a Facilitator can better determine the content of their workshops— this includes activities and structures as mentioned in the previous section. The next step is how you will evaluate the success of your workshop.

Icebreaker

Planning an icebreaker for the workshop is one of the more important steps. It comes close to the end since all of the previous stages have built towards the information required to choose an appropriate activity. Icebreakers help participants relax for the workshop, get to know each other, and better understand the purpose of their writing or the workshop. However, icebreakers are not limited to the beginning of a workshop, as they encourage interaction between participants, between you as the Facilitator and the group, and between you as the Facilitator and the individuals.

Other Materials and Resources

As a final step in planning a workshop, you should use all of the previously acquired information to decide what materials and resources you need to accomplish your tasks. These can range from writing prompts to graphics to background music. Some materials and resources should be gathered beforehand, but others may need to wait until after the icebreaker. Once you have better determined the learning styles of your potential writers, you can better determine what materials will accomplish your objectives.

Writing for Publication

While some writers hone their craft as a hobby or an attempt to improve communication skills, most write with the end goal of publishing their writing— be they creative works or career-related ones. To this end, many participants may seek specific assistance.

In writing for publications, keep in mind the following information:

- **Know the guidelines:** Most publishers have very specific qualities and characteristics they look for in a written work. Make sure the writer knows what sort of work they wish to publish and has a list of at least three publishers that take similar works. If the writer is aiming for a specific publishing company or newspaper, then they can tailor their work to accommodate the guidelines; more often, the writer will complete their manuscript and then find a place that accepts what they have written.
- **Do not worry about perfection:** That is why publishers and newspapers have editors. The most important step is to sit down and write. Most publishers require your manuscript be complete before you submit. Polishing can come after completing a draft.
- **Polish your work:** It does not have to be perfect, but if a manuscript is filled with grammatical errors and typos, then the publishers will most likely pass it up. Remember: most publishers have over 300 manuscripts to read at any given time and only a few open slots for accepting a work. Now is also a good time to get feedback from peers.
- **Review submission guidelines:** Once a manuscript is complete, review where the writer wishes to send it. It helps to read a few other works a publisher has accepted to see if the manuscript is a good match. Writers also want to see how publishers want to receive works:
  - Does the publisher want a few chapters or the whole manuscript?
  - Does the publisher want a query letter or a simple email?
  - Does the publisher ask for a bio? Long or short?
  - Etc.

Tips for submitting a manuscript:
- Be yourself— Do not use a form letter or template
- Be humble but confident

- o KISS – Keep It Short and Sweet
- o Be polite
- o Follow the guidelines
- **Submit, submit, and submit:** Encourage writers to submit their works to more than one place. Make sure they know the guidelines for each and that all of their submissions are unique. Verify that publishers accept simultaneous submissions—if not, then go to each place one at a time.
- **Be prepared to wait:** Publishers have a lot of submissions to go through. It can take a while for them to get to yours. If an editor likes it, then it can take even longer for them to convince their colleagues to accept it.
- **Accept rejection:** Publishers have several reasons for not accepting a manuscript. It may not fit their current specifications, or they may have loved it but it was number eleven out of ten available publishing slots.
  - o Never, ever rebut a rejection: It is highly unprofessional and can put a "black mark" on your name with that—and any affiliated—publication.
  - o It is OK to ask why: Many editors for publications are happy to explain the reason behind a rejection. If you wish to ask, make sure you are polite and understanding in your correspondence.
- **Revise:** Take any feedback from the publisher to make revisions to a work. Not all rejections are final: some will say "we will take this if you work on it in this way."
- **Try again:** Encourage writers to keep at it. Repeat the process as necessary until their work finds its place.
- **Do not give up!**

During the process of preparing for publishing, it is always a good idea to do some legwork and networking. Throughout the year, publishers send representatives to conferences, conventions, and other special events across the country. Get to know these men and women. Talk to them, learn about their companies. The better an impression you leave, the more likely they will remember your name with you make a submission.

Make sure to stress for writers that it is very important to remain polite and professional. The more arrogant or rude they come across, the less likely publishers will give them the time of day. It is not just about the manuscript—it is about the author. A publisher wants to know that the author is someone they can work with and who will work with them. Submission guidelines are a way to test this: does the author know how to follow directions? Do they care enough about our company to understand what we require of them? Do they care enough to have a complete, polished manuscript?

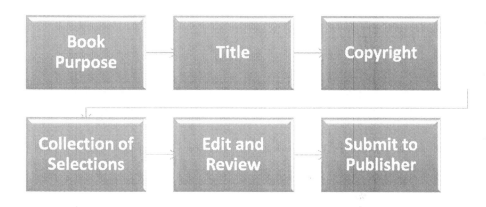

Figure 9.4 Publication Process

Conclusion

Acting as a facilitator can be nerve-wracking but is ultimately rewarding. It is our hope at The Carnegie Writers, Inc. that the information discussed herein will help potential facilitators prepare themselves to act as a guiding force for current and future writers—whether in the creative or business realms. However, even with all of the provided information, you should know that no perfect formula exists for workshop planning.

Workshops vary based on the participants' needs; facilitators should be flexible in order to guide writers.

References

Beder, H., & Darkenwald, G. (1982). Differences between teaching adults and pre-adults: Some propositions and findings. *Adult Education Quarterly*, 142-155.

Gospe, M. (2016). 9 characteristics of a good facilitator. Retrieved from http://www.kickstartall.com/9-characteristics-of-a-good-facilitator/

Knowles, M. (1980). Adult learning processes: Pedagogy and andragogy. *Religious Education*, 202-211.

Pappas (2013). 8 Important Characteristics of Adult Learners. Retrieved from https://elearningindustry.com/8-important-characteristics-of-adult-learners

Nashville Community Education (2016). Retrieved from http://www.nashville.gov/Nashville-Community-Education.aspx

Motivation for Writers:
How to Complete a Writing Project
Tina Murray

Writers write for a variety of reasons. These reasons may include money, passion, purpose, inspiration, acclaim, praise, or even just the challenge of the thing. Writers also undertake many different types of writing projects. They undertake short projects, such as short stories, poems, articles, essays, speeches, and songs, as well as long projects, such as novels, screenplays, and nonfiction books. Nonfiction books may be textbooks, biographies, memoirs, travel journals, self-help guides, historical tomes, cookbooks, or otherwise. Although many writers complete their writing projects, many do not—especially novices. This chapter addresses the concerns of the writer who has begun a writing project but is having trouble completing it.

Regardless of your reasons for writing, and regardless of the type of project you have chosen, the completion of a work is usually a major goal. However, obstacles can and do arise. Sometimes, the achievement of this goal involves such a great commitment of time and energy that a writer becomes discouraged and gives up. Then again, perhaps a writer has a deadline to meet--cannot—and panics. Occasionally, a writer may experience writer's block, that temporary state of mind wherein creative ideas cease to flourish.

For example, the first two or three chapters of a novel may pour forth freely from the writer's mind, and then the flow suddenly stops. The would-be novelist is left with a partially written story and no idea of how to proceed to the finish line. At other times, pressing life events may occur, events which require immediate attention. A writer, drawn away from writing for a period of time, loses focus and feels loathe to return to the project, or even overwhelmed by the prospect of doing so. Various other scenarios are possible, as well.

Every serious writer who has ever set out to accomplish the goal of completing a work—for instance, a book— has experienced at least one setback, often several. A successful writer, however, manages to overcome each setback as it happens and to carry on to ultimate victory. How? By trial and error? Sheer will? To some degree, yes, at first. Eventually, however, a persistent writer becomes seasoned, initiated, even savvy. By gradually learning how to develop and work within your unique creative process, you will gain understanding, skill, and ease.

Such personal mastery involves a synthesis of three primary components. First, you need to understand what actually motivates you as an individual in terms of completing particular projects. Second, you must develop and employ personally effective workaday plans for achieving writing goals. Third, you must learn to cooperate with The Muse. When brought together, these three components—motivation, planning, and understanding the creative process--can arm you with a dynamic, flexible, and productive approach to completing a writing project. At the same time, you may create the best work possible. Each of the three components of this individualized approach will be addressed briefly in the following paragraphs.

The Writer's Motivation

Over the years, scientists have researched motivation in human beings. The approach offered in this chapter, however, is more spiritual than scientific in nature. Many writers struggle with negative thoughts about themselves, thoughts which lead to negative feelings. Negative thoughts and feelings can lead to adverse decision-making, self-censorship, procrastination, and, worst of all, the avoidance of writing altogether. One remedy for this spiritual condition is to take charge of your thoughts (Hay, 1991).

Learning to replace negative thoughts about yourself, and your writing ability, with loving, supportive thoughts can be a career game-changer. In her book *This Time I Dance*, Tama Kieves (2006) details her own experience with fear, regret, and self-doubt as a writer. When describing her inner journey from avoidance of writing and self-blame to self-forgiveness, self-acceptance, and self-encouragement, Kieves wrote, "I had begun to glimpse what it was felt like to have someone on my side inside..."

If you are prone to procrastination or avoidance of writing, a metaphysical approach to inner change may help eliminate such pernicious mind-sets. Although one school of thought promotes the "Just do it" approach to life, inner spiritual work on yourself may provide a kinder, more long-lasting, transformative experience. Additionally, getting to know yourself can be of benefit when exploring your true motivations. Perseverance is easier to muster when you have a meaningful reward in mind and a willing inner cheerleader to encourage self-belief.

As noted previously, writers write for various reasons. Some reasons they admit; some, they do not. They may realize some reasons but be unaware of others. However, when dealing with motivation and what motivates an individual to complete a large, time-consuming, complex task from scratch, you ought to look beyond the apparent. You must dig deep, so to speak. Exploring the not-so-obvious within your psyche requires courage, but it can be a valuable learning experience.

If you want fame, glory, a book deal, or whatever, then your motivation needs to be intense and real—and, frankly, what that motivation *is* does not matter. All that matters is that the specific reward really, really matters to you. Therefore, you should consciously evaluate your inner drive, seeking to determine a specific motivating stimulus that truly stimulates. Then, envision the reward and keep it uppermost in your mind throughout the duration of the writing project. If the mental image or feeling fades, consider creating a vision board and displaying it prominently in the work space. Regular visualizing of goals can help to sustain persistence.

The will to persist until a goal is reached, plus the belief that it can be accomplished, plus the prospect of desired rewards equals a tremendous motivating inner-force. Of course, in certain situations, this navel-gazing may seem impractical and time-consuming—but never fear! Even if you have to forge ahead without doing spiritual work beforehand, such work can be done along the way. More good news: all the subsequent work can be rendered less strenuous if you develop and implement a personalized plan of action.

The Writer's Plan of Action

When you have set an intention to complete a writing project and have determined a uniquely effective impetus, your next step should be to plan a daily writing schedule. This schedule should span the entire estimated duration of the writing project. Each writer's plan will be unique. Some writers will be able to create a work schedule quickly; others, neither quickly nor easily. Physical factors such as environment, space, time, technology, and equipment available weigh heavily when crafting a plan, as do competing factors such as job duties, family obligations, adequate rest, and leisure activities.

The following four-point plan may help the writer who has yet to snatch victory from the jaws of defeat, but who sincerely desires to do so. This plan is merely an example of such procedures, however, not a blueprint. Each writer must experiment, for individual circumstances vary, as do preferences and proclivities. No matter your reason for writing, and no matter what you have set out to write, these four steps offer the promise of hope. When

undertaking a writing project, a writer can:
1. Make a decision to succeed;
2. Develop a work schedule;
3. Implement the work plan; and
4. Reap the ultimate reward.

If this scheme seems daunting, keep in mind that many large life goals require determination, scheduling, time commitment, and hard work. More often than not, they entail delayed gratification of significant rewards. For example, earning a college degree or a professional license takes all of the above. Athletes training for the Olympics devote years of their lives to attainment of goals that may or may not manifest. Even a simple job search requires some element of planning, and a job seeker is motivated by the far-off promise of income.

Completing a large writing project is no different, except in the regard that writing is a creative act, so more is involved in the process than simply following a procedure. Because it requires a sprinkling of fairy dust, it is comparable to learning to dance a ballet or play a violin in a symphony orchestra, competently, until artistry develops. Nothing beats great talent augmented by great skill. The most brilliant pianist begins a lifelong career by practicing the scales, though the overarching goal is to play Chopin in Carnegie Hall. The first step in the development of any skill is to decide that you can and will, no matter what.

Make a decision to succeed
Deciding to believe in your capability—for it is a conscious decision-- is a mighty step forward for any self-doubter (Barker, 1968/2011). In any writing endeavor, self-doubt is tantamount to disaster. Instead of dwelling on thoughts of failure and inadequacy, set an intention to succeed. At this point, motivations can come into play.

After deciding to succeed at completing a writing project, begin with the end goal in mind. What does this mean? It means to use a spiritual technique drawn from the writings of Neville Gardner, who advocated "thinking from the end" as a strategy for ensuring success. Essentially, it is another way of visualizing: "Determined imagination, thinking from the end, is the beginning of all miracles" (Goddard, (1954/2016, p. 2). One of Neville Goddard's devotees, Dr. Wayne Dyer—a prolific author and spiritual leader-- used the strategy to good advantage. Each time he began to write a new book, Dr. Dyer (2012) would create a physical mock-up of the final published book, including the book title on the front cover, and keep it on display at his writing workplace (Dyer). In other words, he proceeded to write with an image of his end goal constantly in view.

Making a decision to complete a writing project and thinking from the end are powerful tools for the writer to employ at the outset of a major job. This entails affirming, "I will finish this writing project—no matter what," thus setting an intention (Dyer, 2012). Avoid indulging in negative self-talk; instead, focus on the exciting writing to come.

Develop a work schedule
Planning the work schedule comprises two separate steps. To begin, the content of the projected work can be outlined. Some writers do not like to work with an outline, but even a rough sketch will help with scheduling time allotments and travel, if required. Once an outline or sketch has been crafted, estimate the necessary time involved for completing the entire project. Divide into daily chunks of hours, weeks, months, allowing for the penciling in of setbacks and hurdles. Then, plot the whole schedule out on a calendar. Use any device. The point is to create a framework.

Such a writing schedule will go a long way towards relieving your anxiety. The regimen itself need not be brutal. In fact, if it is, the regimen may not be realistic. Any sensible writer will not—and should not—follow a schedule that is punishing.

Another suggestion is to plan periodic small rewards into the writing schedule. For example, you might purchase a pair of running shoes or a new outfit at the half-way point. Schedule a glass of wine or tea at the end of each work session. Buy a box of candy each time a chapter is completed— whatever works to give you a psychological advantage. Once the schedule is made, go straight to the business of writing.

Implement the work plan

Now the real creative work of the writing project begins. Your self-discipline and work ethic will be sorely tested during this phase, even if the chosen topic engenders enthusiasm. Hurdles will arise. Setbacks may occur, once you are in place sitting or standing at a work station. The initial decision to complete the project becomes crucial at this time.

All the tools you have crafted and assembled—physically, mentally, spiritually—may be utilized during this phase. The efficacy of physical items such as vision boards, book mock-ups, and incremental rewards will become apparent—or not. Mental tactics, such as visualization of desired outcomes—travel, fame, fortune—may be employed to good use. The spiritual tools—the decision to succeed and the will to persist—will show themselves to be critical, but all the tools are most effective when used in combination. The wise writer will keep an arsenal and add to it as the work of writing continues.

The beauty of scheduling becomes apparent, as well. Able to refer to a pre-conceived plan, you have a roadmap to follow and are not left meandering through a project, wondering what to do next or becoming confused and discouraged. Similarly, the outline or sketch of the work itself allows you to retain more control of the writing process.

The goal is to complete the project, no matter what occurs, so you should allow for adjustments. Make them when necessary. Be neither slack nor a stickler. In the spirit—if not the exact words—of the great Winston Churchill, never give up (Quotations). However, do be flexible.

If a prolonged dry spell occurs, stick to the schedule. If writer's block looms, go to work during regularly scheduled hours anyway. Sit or stand at the work station. Daydream there. Contemplate. Mull. Muse. Converse with your inner cheerleader. Put in the allotted time, and the writing process will right itself. A seasoned writer accepts the inevitability of such periods, takes them in stride, and— remaining optimistic— cooperates with the creative force.

Encouraging yourself through positive self-talk (Hay, 1991) will be, perhaps, the single most significant factor as a writing project progresses to completion. If scheduling is the roadmap, then positive self-talk is the GPS, guiding a writer along said map to ultimate success.

Reap the ultimate rewards
If you have persevered by continually visualizing the end goal, including the rewards to come, have made steady progress according to plan, and have faced and overcome all obstacles and setbacks, then success is imminent. This is the time for self-congratulations!

One note of caution: as you approach the end of a writing project—which, for example, would mean a completed final draft of a book, ready for submission to a publisher—it is important to not overwork your creation. How do you know when a final draft is final? Every creative person faces this question. A painter must paint a last stroke (Lendl, 2014). A composer must craft a final bar. A sculptor must put down the chisel. A filmmaker must approve the final cut. Likewise, a writer must write the words "the end" — and mean it.

Besides, the editor will change things anyway, prior to publication.

The Mysterious Creative Process

During the writing process, the X-factor is the mood of the Muse—and your rolling response to its changes. Although many writers have a capacity for feeling, sensing, and melding into the field of creative energy around them and inside them, a novice writer may not understand what cooperating with the mood of the Muse entails.

Initially, cooperation involves being open to the ideas that come into your mind, seemingly from out of nowhere. It involves learning to receive these ideas without question or judgment at the times they appear. Ideas—thoughts, sentences, fragments, words, dialogue, sounds, images— seemingly drop into the mind from out of nowhere. Whenever they do, it is important to grasp them and record them immediately (Gilbert, 2015). As a writer becomes comfortable, even excited about working within the sense of wonder, a new level of creativity is reached (Murray, 2015).

You will discover that the Muse is not always benevolent. Sometimes, the Muse needs to take a rest or go underground to make vital connections, and the writer is left bereft, straining to create consciously, wondering what to write next. At these times, you need not despair. You will learn to allow for times such as these, when your conscious mind needs to take a break and let the subconscious mind go to work (Fields, 2016).

This does not mean that the world is coming to an end. In fact, it is a natural part of the writing process and must be treated as such. When it happens, instead of giving up, relax. Learn to roll with the creative energy. Trust it, and the tide will eventually turn, probably when least expected.

Realize what is happening and that it is a natural, valuable part of the creative process (Gilbert, 2015). Instead of fretting, go eat at an ice-cream cone. Play a round of golf. Do whatever relaxes you. By clearing the conscious mind before returning to a writing schedule, you will often find that—surprise!—the problem is solved. The subconscious mind—the creative force, the Muse— has worked it out perfectly.

Therefore, learn when to let the subconscious mind take over. It will make connections underground, so to speak, if allowed to do so (Fields, 2016). This other-worldly aspect of creativity ought to be factored—or perhaps, absorbed by osmosis— into each and every writer's working knowledge of art and craft, especially those who work within the realm of fiction.

The beauty of this technique is that an experienced writer will begin to recognize these energy changes, deliberately using them to advantage and not feeling threatened by them. This is a learned skill—learned, once you realize what is happening: the creative force wants to create through the writer (Gilbert) and it needs the writer's cooperation to so. Be willing to follow that inner voice's lead. Be willing to listen, accept, and flow. Often, the results of such a practice prove to be better than the results produced by self-conscious agonizing. By learning to work in tandem with the creative process, rather than in opposition to it, you advance towards fulfillment.

One final note on creativity: if the tripartite approach described in this chapter seems too clinical, antiseptic, or even sterile, remember the credo of art educators across the land: "Creativity is messy." As well it should be! Creative writing, like art, is not some tidy sweeping up of disparate details. Yes, it requires technique. Yes, its aim is order; but that is the writer's job: to bring order out of creative chaos. Chaos before order.

Indeed, writing a book can be—and on some level, should be—a messy process. In her award-winning weekly newsletter, *Funds for Writers,* C. Hope Clark (2014) included a quotation attributed to H. L. Mencken: "Writing books is certainly a most unpleasant occupation. It is lonesome, unsanitary, and maddening. Many authors go crazy."

Amusing, yes; however, a courageous writer best not ignore the sentiment behind Mencken's words. Fortunately, all becomes worthwhile once the final chapter is written.

All Together Now

Taken together, the components of this tripartite approach can lead to a predictable outcome: a completed writing project. Happily, an unexpected outcome may result as well: you gain control! You become creatively empowered, now possessing a skill set, transferable to new and varied writing projects. Although each separate part of this approach may be beneficial in and of itself, the totality of the approach may result in new power and artistic control. Thus, the approach has a Gestalt-like quality. Gestalt is defined as "a configuration, pattern, or organized field having specific properties that cannot be derived from the summation of its component parts; a unified whole" (Dictionary.com, n.d.) This quality underscores the importance of at least giving the approach, in its entirety, a try. Utilizing it may enable you to reach performance outcomes beyond expectations, especially as more and more experience accumulates and individualized adjustments are made. Potentially, what may result for a writer utilizing this approach is new creative competence, command, and virtuosity.

Conclusion

The approach suggested here is not the only way to tackle and complete a writing project. However, if you are having difficulty bringing a work into being, serious consideration should be given to this approach and subsequent experimentation with it. Mend it. Mold it. Bend it. Break it. Never forget that "[o]ur power lies in our ability to make ourselves do that which we desire to do" (Rugen, 2016). If applied, this approach can help one to do just that.

Now, go finish that book.

References

Barker, R. C. (1968/2011). *The power of decision: A step-By-step program to overcome indecision and live without failure forever.* CITY STATE Penguin. Originally published 1968.

Clark, C. H. (2014). *Funds for Writers newsletter, (14, 22).*

Dyer, W. (2012). *Wishes fulfilled* [Television broadcast]. Nashville, TN: Public Broadcasting System.

Fields, J. (2016). From presentation to Carnegie Writers' Group: *Writer's Block.* Nashville Public Library, Green Hills Branch; Nashville, TN.

Gestalt. (n.d.). *Dictionary.com.* Retrieved from http://www.dictionary.com/browse/gestalt

Gilbert, E. (2016). *Choosing curiosity over fear: On being.* National Public Radio. (2015).

Goddard, N. (1954/2016.) Awakened imagination. (Retrieved from http://www.awakenedimaginationandthesearch.org; Chapter 2, p. 2. (Awakened Imagination /Includes The Search, originally published by DeVorss and Company, 1-1-1954.) p.1.

Hay, L. (1991). The power is within you. *CITY STATE* Hay House.

Kieves, T. (2006). This time I dance. New York, New *York.* Tarcher/Perigee/Penguin.

Lendl, A. (2014, February 2). When is an artwork finished? *ART News.* Retrieved from http://www.artnews.com/2014/02/24/when-is-an-artwork-finished/

Murray, T. (2015). A sense of wonder: Why every creative writer needs one. *Enhancing Writing Skills.* Charlotte, North Carolina. Information Age Publishing.

Rugen, N. B. (2016). Personal Communication.

Winston, C. (n.d.) Quotations. *Winston Churchill.org.* Retrieved from www.winstonchurchill.org/resources/quotations

Creating Characters
with Depth and Dimension
Jaden Terrell

The Importance of Character

When I was in the third grade, I read a book called *The Silver Sword* by Ian Serraillier. I carried this book everywhere with me, reading and re-reading it until it crumbled in my hand. I still remember tears streaming down my eight-year-old face as the Nazis invaded Poland and shattered the Balicki family.

Forty-plus years later, I am still haunted by responsible Ruth, irrepressible Bronia, determined Edek, and orphaned Jan, who feared there would be no place for him once the family was reunited. Serraillier never said Ruth was responsible; he showed me through her care for those she loved. He never said Edek was determined; he showed me a boy whose desire to find and protect his sisters was so strong that he escaped a Nazi prison camp by clinging to the underbelly of a train for hours; and rather than telling me about Jan's fears, he showed me through the boy's jealous behavior toward Edek and his possessiveness of the girls.

Think of the books you love most. Is it not the characters who made them memorable? What happens, though, when you pick up a book and the characters are flat? Inconsistent? Unlikable? Boring? I once read a book about a group of people traveling through multiple dimensions on a modified sewing machine. The characters were so unpleasant, flat, and interchangeable that, fifty pages in, I wished they would all just die and be done with it. I could not even finish the book.

Let me start by saying no one way to create a great character is best, just as no one way to write a novel exists. Every writer has his or her own processes and techniques, and while you can always learn from other writers, you must ultimately figure out what works for you. Personally, I like to get to know my characters before I start. Even though there is still plenty to discover along the way, knowing who they are and what motivates them can drive the story and add depth and dimension.

The strategies and techniques I am about to give you are not ironclad rules. They are just tools. Use them as you see fit. I will alternate between male and female pronouns. When you use the questions, adjust according to the sex of your character. Not all of this information will find its way into your book, but your answers will nonetheless inform the character's worldview and actions.

The Foundation

Character creation is one of the most fascinating and important parts of writing fiction. Much of the process involves asking yourself questions. The first one is, "What do you already know about your book?" You might already have a main character. Perhaps you know you want to write a cozy mystery, thriller, police procedural, romance, fantasy, or literary novel. Maybe you already have a plot sketched out, or maybe you just have an image, like the one of a little girl in muddy underpants that gave birth to William Faulkner's *The Sound and the Fury* (New York Times, 2004).

However much or little you know about your book, you will answer subsequent questions about your main character within the context of what you have already decided. If you make a choice that fails to mesh with your previous decisions, you must either change one or more of your earlier choices or figure out how to make the incompatibility work in your favor.

Imagine you want to write a gritty, high-tech thriller with lots of violence and explosions. A frail, near-sighted beekeeper with sciatica whose hobby is stamp-collecting and who is so technologically challenged he does not even own a computer or a cell phone would be an unlikely protagonist. But what if you are married to both these ideas? First, you will need to give your beekeeper a reason to get involved in your thriller plot (perhaps he saw something he should not have, which puts him in the crosshairs of a dangerous criminal organization), a motivation to continue (now his life or the life of a loved one is in danger), and a believable means of overcoming his physical limitations (perhaps with the help of a secondary character who does possess the necessary skills). He should find a way to use his knowledge of bees, stamps, or sciatica to overcome or outwit the villains.

He must have strengths he never knew he possessed, and the reader will need to see a hint of those strengths early in the story. While you can write a great book by going against expectations, it may take some work to make it believable.

If you already know your setting and genre, you need to make sure your character could exist (and function) in that setting. If you know parts of your plot, your character must be able to do what is necessary to carry that plot.

Another thing to take into account is whether you are writing a series or a standalone novel. If your book is a romance, you are probably writing a standalone. Other genres, like mystery and thriller, lend themselves equally well to either. Many literary novels are standalones; the book covers the single defining, life-changing event in the character's life. To revisit that character at any other point in his or her life would be anticlimactic.

A series character should also undergo changes, but within a single book, these changes may be relatively small. Instead, although each book stands alone, a greater story arc covers the entire series. Think of Lawrence Block's Matthew Scudder. While Scudder reacts to the events of each book, the major changes of his life take place over the course of the series. He acknowledges his alcoholism, joins AA, and learns to control his urge to drink. He dates a series of women, falls in love with a former prostitute, marries her, and begins to reconcile (after a fashion) with the adult sons of his first marriage. If all that happened in a single book, then where would he have left to go? After only a few books, he would be unrecognizable.

If you envision a series, your main character needs to be a multi-faceted character with enough complications and entanglements to sustain a reader's interest for the long haul. It is especially important that your protagonist is someone you like well enough to invest a hefty chunk of time with. Will you like this character enough to live with him or her for a decade or longer? As we go through the character creation process together, remember: nothing is carved in stone. You can always change your mind later if a better idea comes to you.

Your Protagonist

Can you imagine Miss Marple, Agatha Christie's iconic amateur sleuth, slugging it out with a hopped-up pimp in a shadowy alley that smells of urine and rotting garbage? Can you imagine Mike Hammer, Mickey Spillane's hardboiled private detective, sipping tea in a parson's parlor, quietly ruminating about the psychological foibles of a small-town microcosm of society? Well, maybe you can—writers live on imagination—but the image fails to hold up over the long haul. Poor Miss Marple would end up with a cut throat or a broken hip, and Mike Hammer would punch out the parson, and the balance of the universe would be restored. The characters must be true to the story—and vice versa.

The most important character in your novel is your protagonist. Why? Because, while the antagonist's actions may drive the story, it is the protagonist your readers should be most invested in, the one they have to care enough about to follow for the duration of a book or several books. In a crime novel, your protagonist is generally the character who solves the mystery or foils the villain's diabolical plans. A romance often features two protagonists, the two halves of the couple, with approximately half the chapters from each person's point of view (POV). In a fantasy, the main character is the one who carries the primary burden of solving the book's most essential problem; J.R.R. Tolkien's fantasy masterpiece *Lord of the Rings* has many important characters, but Frodo is the protagonist. If you already know what kind of book you are writing, you already know a few things about the main character.

If you know your novel is a cozy mystery set in a small New England town, then you can already rule out a few characteristics. Since this subgenre typically features an amateur sleuth, you know your character is not a police officer or other law enforcement official. She is neither foul-mouthed nor brutal. She is curious enough and courageous enough to try and solve a crime most people would leave to the police.

Remember to keep the tone of the book in mind. In a light or cozy story, the protagonist will have flaws and a history, but her baggage should not be too heavy. She might bite her nails, but she is probably not addicted to heroin. She might have a strained relationship with her mother, but she probably was not locked in a closet for days and then beaten with coat hangers. On the other hand, if your book is a gritty psychological thriller, you need a character with the skills to defeat a cunning and dangerous killer. Her background and emotional life may be darker and more complex.

Each choice you make narrows your future choices. A tightrope walker is unlikely to also be clumsy; if he is, you must explain why he chose such an unlikely profession and how he manages to both keep his job and avoid being splattered all over ring three. By eliminating choices or making (and explaining) unlikely ones, you begin to get a clearer picture of your character. Later, this will help you with plotting.

The following discussion and questions assume a modern-day setting. If you are writing a historical novel, fantasy, or science fiction, adapt the questions to match the time period and the world you've built.

The Basics: Sex, Age, Appearance, Setting

First, is the character male or female? Men and women are often treated very differently. They may have different ways of communicating and different priorities. They are subject to different gender expectations. Whether they conform to or rebel against those expectations reflects their individual characters. Now, add in all the permutations of sexuality and gender identification and all each entails, and you can see that biological sex, cultural expectations, gender identification, and life experiences related to all of the above play a huge role in shaping a person's character.

How old is the character? Wet behind the ears? Middle-aged and clinging to youth? Grizzled and wizened? Picture a young man fresh out of college hired to manage a group of older men near retirement. Would they resent him? Be afraid of the changes he might implement? Now, imagine the opposite: an older, newly divorced woman going to college after spending the past twenty-five years as a mother and housewife. How would she and her much younger classmates navigate the differences in age and experience? Age affects a character's perceptions, life experience, and physicality. It affects how the character is perceived by others, which in turn affects other dynamics in your story.

What does your character look like? Some writers choose to leave the character's appearance vague so the reader can create the character in his or her own image, but even if you choose not to put these details on the page, you should know them yourself. Why? Because how we look affects how people respond to us. It affects how we perceive ourselves and what we expect from other people.

A prime example of this is Jack Reacher, the massively built hero of Lee Child's bestselling thriller series. Jack's sheer physical size is the first thing people notice about him. It gives him an advantage in some situations, a disadvantage in others. It influences his tactical decision-making. A short, small-boned man, even one with the same level of skill and training, would approach the same situations in a very different way.

I cannot emphasize enough the psychological effects of physical appearance. Imagine two women in a café. "Emma" is tall and slender, a woman who has always been beautiful in all the ways our society defines beauty. An expensive dress, expensive jewelry, and flawless makeup complete the picture. "Sybil," on the other hand, has plain features, acne-pitted skin, lank shapeless hair, Coke-bottle glasses, and a worn sweat suit stretched tight over rolls of fat. How do you think the servers and the other customers respond to each woman? How does each one carry herself? Imagine the gestures and other body language each woman might use as she interacts with a man she finds attractive or a surly salesperson at a high-end boutique. Each of these women perceives the world through the filter of her own experiences, which in turn affect her attitudes, behaviors, and social interactions.

Now, imagine a third woman, Claire. By all objective standards, she could be a super model. But she was a plain, awkward teenager whose parents belittled her and whose classmates teased her about her appearance. The world sees her as an

Emma, but inside, she still sees herself as a Sybil. That self-image will affect all of her interactions and relationships.

Knowing how your character lives is also important. Where does she live? Does she own her house? Rent an apartment? Sleep on her mother's couch? Is she a neatnik, a slob, or something in between? What kind of security precautions does she take? Where did she grow up? Did she stay near home, or did she get as far as away as she could? Why? The answers to these questions can reveal a great deal about your protagonist. For example, one of my characters, Kit Cohen, grew up with a mother who was constantly uprooting her. Each time they would leave one of her mother's husbands, Kit and her mother would each pack a small suitcase with clothing and a single box of favorite belongings. When they arrived at their new apartment, they would show each other what they had brought—the things each considered "box-worthy." As a result, Kit guards against becoming too attached to anyone or anything. Now that she has her own home, she is torn between filling it with disposable items, painless to lose, and filling it only with items she finds box-worthy.

Think about your own story. Is your character attractive or plain? Athletic or unfit? How does he dress? Where and how does he live? Growing up, was he the kid picked last on the playground, or was he the captain of the team? All of these things will affect his image of himself, as well as how others respond to him.

Profession, Hobbies, Interests, and Special Abilities

Many of your character's skills are dictated by (or reflected in) his or her profession. If particular skills are needed in order for your plot to work, consider giving your character a profession in which she would have had an opportunity to either learn those skills or meet someone who has them.

For example, in a thriller or hard-edged mystery, you might choose a professional investigator (perhaps a police officer, federal agent, private detective, or corporate spy) or someone who works in a technological field. A cozy or traditional mystery is more likely to feature an amateur sleuth. Cozy novels have been written about herbalists, cheese makers, chefs, and quilters, among other things. Often, knowledge gained through this profession is critical to solving the crime.

Think about the skills your novel requires. If your romance novel requires your characters to tangle over ancient Japanese artifacts, maybe at least one of them is a museum curator or a historian specializing that time period. If your mystery hinges on the sleuth's understanding of jellyfish behavior, perhaps she should be an oceanographer. Hobbies, interests, and special abilities may affect the plot as well. For example, an expert in beadwork might notice if a supposedly wealthy suspect is wearing a necklace made of cheap imitation glass beads, rather than the expensive crystal beads one would expect.

Areas of lack may also provide interesting plot developments. Kit Cohen, for example, has never used a weapon and never wants to. When a fight erupts and her date is being strangled, she breaks up the fight by dumping a pitcher of ice water down the aggressor's collar. In this case, her lack of special abilities forces her to rely on this pedestrian solution. How much easier it would have been for her (and how much worse for the plot) if she knew how to use a Vulcan death grip.

Social Connections and Relationships

When I started writing my private detective series, I knew what my protagonist, Jared McKean, *looked* like—mid-thirties, buckskin-colored hair, Marlboro-man good looks. I knew he came from a law enforcement background and that he wore a leather bomber jacket that his father had worn in Vietnam, but these were surface characteristics. Only after I began to explore his relationships with others did he really come to life.

As I asked myself questions about his relationships, a pattern emerged. Jared has a 36-year-old Quarter Horse he has had since he was a boy. He has an elderly Akita. He is still in love with his ex-wife. His housemate and landlord is a gay man with AIDS, a man Jared has been friends with since kindergarten. Laying out these relationships showed me a key aspect of Jared's character: this man does not let go of the things he loves. This characteristic is a driving force in the Jared McKean books, and I might not have discovered it if I had not taken the time to explore his relationships.

If you would like to use relationships to add more depth and complexity to your protagonist, ask yourself about her relationships with the people in her life. Is she married? Single, divorced, or widowed? If married, what is her relationship with her spouse like? If divorced, what caused the dissolution of the marriage? If she is widowed, under what circumstances?

Decide whether or not the character has a child or children. Then think about the relationship the character has with each child. Remember, children have to be taken care of, so if your character has any, the care and nurturing of those children must be taken into account when you create your plot. If, for example, your homicide detective, a single mother, has to spend a week on a stakeout, you will have to consider, not only who will care for her children in her absence but her own feelings about being away from them for so long.

Go through this same process with the character's other important relationships, such as those with close friends, allies, and other family members. Be sure to consider any emotional conflicts and the implications of these relationships, including the possibility of relationships in which a friend, family member, or ally is also a rival. In these circumstances, how does the character balance love and tension, or love and betrayal?

Each time you answer a question, you learn more about the character. As before, each choice you make narrows the possibilities of future choices. Each new choice must be consistent with what has come before. Otherwise, you should go back and reconcile the apparent contradiction. For example, if your character is charming and charismatic with his colleagues but cold and emotionally controlling with his spouse, you need to understand why and help your readers understand as well.

Eliminating choices or making and explaining unlikely ones gives you a clearer picture of the character. By surrounding that character with people who bring out different facets of his or her personality, you end up with a main character of depth and complexity—one your readers will remember long after they have closed the cover of your book.

Looking for Patterns

Are you beginning to see any patterns? Do you feel like you are getting to know your character? Are you beginning to see her strengths? Her flaws or weaknesses? How she interacts with others? Keep asking questions. You can answer them in either first or third person.

For example, if the question is, "What was your worst birthday experience?" you might write:

> On Ronald's fourteenth birthday, the head cheerleader, on whom he had a huge crush, sent him a perfumed note asking him to meet her behind the bleachers. When he got there, the entire cheerleading squad was there laughing at him.

Or you might say:

> In the ninth grade, I had this huge crush on the head cheerleader. Her name was Allison. Allison Linley. On my fourteenth birthday, as we were leaving homeroom, she slipped a note into my sweaty palm. The note smelled like flowers. "Meet me behind the bleachers after fourth period," it said. I couldn't believe it. I practically floated down to the football field that afternoon. Never mind that I'd be late for Mrs. Pinchley's Algebra class and would probably have to write 'I will not skip class' nine thousand times. I was in love. When I got there, she was standing beside the concession stand. The rest of the cheerleading squad was gathered around her, and they were all laughing and pointing at me. "Oh, Ronald," Allison said. "You're such a dork." I've never asked a woman out that I didn't think about that day and break out in a cold sweat.

You will discover other things about the character as your story progresses, so leave yourself room for surprises. A long-lost cousin? A secret sibling? Time will tell.

Desires, Drives, Obstacles, and Conflicts

By now, you have learned a lot about your main character, from physical appearance to habits and preferences. You have thought about strengths, weaknesses, and defining moments. The next step is to go deeper, to find out what really makes your character tick, then talk about how to use what you have learned to give your story more power and depth.

A character's conscious desires and unconscious drives work together to determine his or her actions in the face of obstacles and conflicts. These four elements—desires, drives, obstacles, and conflicts—can help shape your plot and determine the course of your story. To make sure we are all on the same page, we will begin by discussing what these terms mean.

Desires
Desires are those things we are consciously aware that we want. Vonnegut (2011) said, "Every character should want something, even if it's just a glass of water." Why? Because tension is created when something stands between the character and the thing she wants, and it is tension that keeps readers turning pages.

Drives
In this context, drives are unconscious motivations. Some neuroscientists believe that 95-99% of human behavior is determined by unconscious processes (Bargh & Morsella, 2008). The mind is like an iceberg, with the tip made up of conscious thoughts and awareness and the rest—by far the largest part— beneath the surface. Although it remains unseen, it is the foundation that holds everything else up. Some say the unconscious mind is like a computer or a tape recorder, playing back the same old messages over and over. Others say it is roiling, chaotic, primordial soup. Whichever image you prefer, this much we know is true: it remembers everything we have ever experienced and everything we ever felt about those experiences.

When new situations arise, the unconscious mind sifts through those old experiences, finds something similar to this new situation, and uses that past experience to tell us what to think and feel about what is happening now. We make our decisions based on thoughts and emotions lurking down there in the primordial ooze. Then we justify them based on rational thoughts and logic.

Imagine little Teddy, five years old. He marches off to kindergarten, where he learns the alphabet and how those 26 letters are magically transformed into words. One afternoon, sitting at the kitchen table, he writes a story about a squirrel and a spaceship. His brother looks over his shoulder and laughs. "That's the stupidest thing I ever read. Squirrels can't drive spaceships. Plus, you can't even spell." Teddy crumples his story and throws it in the trash. Why did he ever think "Squirrels in Space" was a good idea?

Grade 3 comes, and the class bully laughs at Teddy's story about a time-traveling T-Rex. Grade 7, and the teacher reads his report on Napoleon aloud to the class—as an example of how not to write a report. Later, in the hall, everybody looks at him and snickers. And so it goes. Teddy grows up to be Ted. He hates his English classes; he finds them boring and stupid. Instead, he gets a degree in business, lands a terrific job, and becomes a rising star in his company. Everything is perfect. Then his supervisor offers him a promotion, with more money, better benefits, and opportunities for advancement. It sounds perfect—except for one thing. He will have to write copy for clients. His unconscious mind knows this a bad idea. While he does not consciously think about the "Squirrels in Space" incident, deep inside, his unconscious mind has already decided that this is a dangerous situation, one Ted must be protected from at all costs.

Ted goes home and makes a list of pros and cons. He thinks of all the rational reasons why the cons carry more weight than the pros. Then he goes back into the office and turns down the position. His decision is based not on his carefully constructed list of pros and cons but on an inner drive to avoid the kind of pain he felt the day his brother laughed at "Squirrels in Space."

Drives are the reasons we want what we want and fear what we fear. They might motivate us to enter a marathon and push on until we drop, even when common sense says we should stop. The conscious desire is to win a medal, get in shape, make Dad proud. The unconscious drive is the fear of not being good enough (because Dad, who was a track star in high school, always let you know when you fell short but never once expressed his approval); a hunger for attention (because when you were small, everyone you knew praised you for your athletic prowess, and that felt *good*); or the need for validation (because your older sister was a star athlete who got all the accolades while you were the clumsy one who sat in the bleachers and pretended to cheer).

Think about your character's unconscious drives and motivations. What influences are working on him that he is not even aware of?

Obstacles and Conflicts
Obstacles and Conflicts are the things that come between your character and what she wants. For the purposes of this lesson, obstacles are external forces (like poverty, natural disasters, physical disabilities or limitations, or an antagonist with opposing drives and desires) while conflicts are internal or interpersonal.

With internal conflict, your character feels opposing emotions (like the desire to win a show jumping competition with a $10,000 prize versus a fear of riding developed after a bad fall from her horse) or is torn between two equally attractive but mutually exclusive options (think of Janet Evanovich's series character Stephanie Plum and her ongoing flirtations with Joe Morelli and Ranger).

Remember that show jumping competition? If your character, Molly, wants to win the competition, has the means to enter, and has no doubts about either entering the competition or about her ability to win, then you have no conflict. Tension is low because nothing is keeping her from getting what she wants. Now, imagine she needs the $10,000 to help pay her way to the college of her dreams, and her best friend, Pia, is also entering the competition. Pia is riding a horse she loves, but the owner (their trainer) is about to sell him, and her foster parents either cannot afford him or are unwilling to buy him for her. Pia is a lonely girl whose only friends are Molly and this horse. Losing him will break her heart. That $10,000 would be enough to buy him. If Molly were to withdraw, Pia would be a shoe-in. Does Molly choose college for herself or happiness for her friend?

Now you have conflict.

Interpersonal conflict occurs when two characters have opposing desires. Some writers think that, to have conflict, the characters have to bicker throughout the story, but that is not the case. Imagine a mother and son. The son wants to go to college, but he knows his widowed mother needs him at home to work in the family business. She has health problems and medical bills. If he leaves, she loses the business and probably her home. He tells her he has decided to forget about college. His mother, on the other hand, wants him to go away to school. She thinks that will provide his best chance for a good future doing work he loves. She tells him she intends to sell the business, sell the house, and get a smaller place. She might even go live in a retirement home. No, he says, she loves this house. He wants her to be able to keep it. There is conflict because their desires are in opposition. Each wants the other to be happy and is willing to sacrifice much to achieve that end. Neither wants the other to make that sacrifice. Can you see how a conversation between these two, in which she tries to convince him to leave despite his determination to stay, could be infused with tension, even though these people are not angry or even annoyed with each other? Even though they are coming from a place of love and mutual respect, their conflicting desires create tension.

Some situations serve as both obstacles and conflicts. Antagonism or rivalry between two characters could be an obstacle (if it results in one keeping the other from a desired outcome), an internal conflict (if it causes emotional turmoil), and an interpersonal conflict (if one confronts the other). Whether internal or interpersonal, though, conflicts are emotionally charged. As a result, they can create powerful moments in your novel.

The Thing Your Character Would Never Do

To get to the heart of your character's internal conflict, agent and writing teacher extraordinaire Donald Maass suggests the following exercise in his book *Writing the Breakout Novel* (2001). Ask yourself: What is something your character would never do? Based on what you know about his motivations and desires, what would make him do that thing? Is there a way to work this into the book? (Maass. 2001)

The mistake I made when I first tried to answer these last two questions was to go with the easy, obvious thing: my character would never rape a woman, murder a child, torture an infant. Nothing was going to make him do those things, and any situation that would make him even consider it would be so extreme as to be implausible.

If you are having the same problem, back away from these most extreme circumstances. If your character is afraid of heights, maybe the thing she would never do would be to cross a suspension bridge over a canyon. What would make her do that? (In one of my workshops, a participant said, "She's not going over that bridge, no matter what!" Not even the thought of a thug with a knife at her character's daughter's throat could budge her. Can you imagine the character's "dark night of the soul" as she watches her daughter die, knowing her fear kept her from saving her child?)

If your answer is "She would never torture anyone," can you think of a circumstance where she might? What if the villain has buried her spouse alive, the clock is ticking, and the captured villain refuses to reveal the spouse's location? Maybe she would, in fact, resist the temptation to torture the information out of the villain, but the conflict between her moral decision not to torture and her desire to save a loved one could make for a powerful scene.

As you develop scenes and plot points, ask yourself how one or more of these elements might add tension and propel the action. Whatever your plotline, the interplay between desires, drives, obstacles, and conflicts can add depth and dimension to your story.

Supporting Cast

Unless you are writing a book like Gary Paulsen's *Hatchet*, which has only one character, your novel will need to be populated by other characters. There may be allies, confidantes, sidekicks, adversaries, rivals. If your book is a mystery, there will be suspects and a victim. Whatever your genre, there is also an antagonist.

An antagonist is not always a villain. The antagonist is simply the person whose own goals and actions make it difficult for the protagonist to achieve his. The animal rights activist who wants to preserve wolves in the area where the struggling farmer lives may be a wonderful, loving person, but if she achieves her goal, it will be at the farmer's expense. His family and livelihood are threatened by the wolves, which kill their livestock. They are already struggling to make ends meet. If this is his story, the activist is the antagonist. If it is her story, he is. The villain/antagonist is the hero of his own story.

Some of these characters will need to be more developed than others. You can use the same process you used with your protagonist to greater or lesser degrees. Even the most minor characters, though, should have at least one or two distinguishing characteristics to keep them from seeming generic and thus detracting from the believability of the story.

A Final Word

By now, you probably have a nicely developed protagonist. But one thing still remains: to show your character in action. According to screenwriter Martin Roth, it is time to get your character up a tree and throw rocks at him. It is through action that your character reveals himself and shows your readers what he is made of.

Helen Keller may have expressed it best when she said, "Character cannot be developed in ease and quiet. Only through experience of trial and suffering can the soul be strengthened, vision cleared, ambition inspired, and success achieved." (Quotes.net, 2016). The same is true for those who begin their lives as letters on a page.

References

Bargh, J. A., and Morsella, E. (2008.) The unconscious mind. *Perspectives on Psychological Science.* Jan. 3(1): 73-79.

Block, L. (1976-2011). *Matthew scudder series.* New York, NY: Various Publishers.

Child, L. (1997). *The killing floor.* New York, NY: G.P. Putnam.

Christie, A. (2004). *Nemesis.* (Reprint edition). New York, NY: William Morris.

Evanovich, J. (1999). *One for the money.* New York NY: Scribner.

Faulkner, W. (1929, 1946). *The sound and the fury.* New York, NY: McGraw Hill.

Keller, H. (n.d.) Helen Keller Quotes. *Quotes.net.* Retrieved July 14, 2016, from http://www.quotes.net/quote/5956.

Maass, D. (2001). *Writing the breakout novel.* Cincinnati, OH: Writer's Digest Books.

Serraillier, I. (2002). *The silver sword.* New York, NY: Vintage Children's Classics.

Spillane, M. (2001). *The mike hammer collection.* New York, NY: New American Library/Penguin.

Tolkien, J.R.R. (1987). *The lord of the rings.* (Reprint edition). New York, NY: Houghton Mifflin.

Writers on writing, Volume II: More Collected Essays from The New York Times. (2004). New York, NY: Times Books

Vonnegut, Kurt. 2011. *Bagombo Snuff Box.* New York, NY: RosettaBooks.

Constructing Better Fiction
Using the Building Blocks of Nonfiction
Kay Gragg

As a retired teacher of English/Language Arts and a lifelong reader, I cannot help but use the construction metaphor as it relates to the writing process. Before you start building a house, you must have a plan. Then, you pour a solid foundation, add supporting walls and ceiling beams, and finally add a roof to "dry it in" so that you can complete the finishing touches to the interior. Likewise, when I taught students how to write an effective composition, I always started with the formulaic five-paragraph model: the essay should begin with an introduction which includes the thesis, followed by three body paragraphs that offer the main supports for the thesis, and a final conclusion. The same basic premise also applies to fiction since it has a beginning, middle, and end. In teaching students to analyze fiction, I supplied them with a graphic organizer for plot structure which required that they identify the exposition, conflict, rising action, climax, falling action, and resolution. This is, of course, a back-ended approach, since it applies to a completed work of fiction, but it serves as a visual representation.

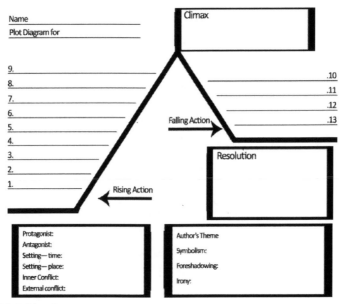

Figure 12.1. Plot Structure

By way of review, let us be sure we understand the literary terms used above as they apply to fiction. The *exposition* is the nonfiction equivalent of an introduction. In it, the writer provides necessary background information about the characters and their circumstances. Often times, the setting in which the narrative takes place is revealed, and foreshadowing may be utilized to hint at future events. Not until a conflict arises can there be any rising action, as the protagonist must struggle against either internal or external factors, or both. As this struggle manifests itself in the narrative, the action continues to build to a turning point, or climax. At that point, the loose ends of the plot begin to be resolved, leading to the story's conclusion.

I am certainly not suggesting that writers of fiction follow these precise steps in constructing a story. The beginning seeds for a story are as varied as there are storytellers. It may start with a character or a situation or a memory from a particular place and time; the writer may not even know at first what will happen or how the story will end as it takes on a life of its own. The creative process probably more closely resembles a cluster diagram than a traditional pyramid, but by the time the piece of fiction, whether it is a short story or a full-blown novel, takes shape, these basic elements have found their way into the narrative structure.

Exposition as Foundation

Have you ever started reading a novel only to discover a few pages in that you have absolutely no interest in the characters or what happens to them? As writers, we must always be cognizant of the need to engage the reader. Doing so requires "dangling the carrot," so to speak, in order to make the reader want to know more. In laying the foundation of my story, the exposition, I am not writing a composition where I need to state the point of my story or take a stance in the opening paragraph. Nor am I writing a news story in which the *who, what, where, when, why*, and *how* are all spelled out in the lead paragraph. Indeed, the exposition of a fictional piece may unfold over the first few pages of a short story or over multiple chapters at the beginning of a novel. Let us examine the opening paragraphs of several works of fiction to see what the writers have chosen to reveal about setting, mood, and character. (Note: *Tone* and *mood* are often used interchangeably; however, they differ slightly in meaning. *Tone* is defined as the speaker's attitude toward the subject, while *mood* is the emotional effect that the text creates for the reader.)

> During the whole of a dull, dark, and soundless day in the autumn of the year, when the clouds hung oppressively low in the heavens, I had been passing alone, on horseback, through a singularly dreary tract of country; and at length found myself, as the shades of the evening drew on, within view of the melancholy House of Usher. I know not how it was — but, with the first glimpse of the building, a sense of insufferable gloom pervaded my spirit. I say insufferable; for the feeling was unrelieved by any of that half-pleasurable, because poetic, sentiment, with which the mind usually receives even the sternest natural images of the desolate or

terrible. I looked upon the scene before me — upon the mere house, and the simple landscape features of the domain — upon the bleak walls — upon the vacant eye-like windows — upon a few rank sedges — and upon a few white trunks of decayed trees — with an utter depression of soul which I can compare to no earthly sensation more properly than to the after-dream of the reveller upon opium — the bitter lapse into every-day life — the hideous dropping off of the veil. There was an iciness, a sinking, a sickening of the heart — an unredeemed dreariness of thought which no goading of the imagination could torture into aught of the sublime. What was it — I paused to think — what was it that so unnerved me in the contemplation of the House of Usher? It was a mystery all insoluble; nor could I grapple with the shadowy fancies that crowded upon me as I [page 292:] pondered. I was forced to fall back upon the unsatisfactory conclusion, that while, beyond doubt, there *are* combinations of very simple natural objects which have the power of thus affecting us, still the analysis of this power lies among considerations beyond our depth. It was possible, I reflected, that a mere different arrangement of the particulars of the scene, of the details of the picture, would be sufficient to modify, or perhaps to annihilate its capacity for sorrowful impression; and, acting upon this idea, I reined my horse to the precipitous brink of a black and lurid tarn that lay in unruffled lustre by the dwelling, and gazed down — but with a shudder even more thrilling than before — upon the re-modelled and inverted images of the gray sedge, and the ghastly tree-stems, and the vacant and eye-like windows.

> —Edgar Allan Poe, "Fall of the House of Usher" (1839)

It was the best of times, it was the worst of times, it was the age of wisdom, it was the age of foolishness, it was the epoch of belief, it was the epoch of incredulity, it was the season of Light, it was the season of Darkness, it was the spring of hope, it was the winter of despair, we had everything before us, we had nothing before us, we were all going direct to Heaven, we were all going direct the other way- in short, the period was so far like the present period, that some of its noisiest authorities insisted on its being received, for good or for evil, in the superlative degree of comparison only.

 There were a king with a large jaw and a queen with a plain face, on the throne of England; there were a king with a large jaw and a queen with a fair face, on the throne of France. In both countries it was clearer than crystal to the lords of the State preserves of loaves and fishes, that things in general were settled for ever.

> —Charles Dickens, *Tale of Two Cities* (1859)

It was a Motel 6 on I-80 just west of Lincoln, Nebraska. The snow that began at midafternoon had faded the sign's virulent yellow to a kinder pastel shade as the light ran out of the January dusk. The wind was closing in on that quality of empty amplification one encounters only in the country's flat midsection, usually in wintertime. That meant nothing but discomfort now, but if the snow came tonight---the weather forecasters couldn't seem to make up their minds---then the interstate would be shut down by morning. That was nothing to Alfie Zimmer.

> —Stephen King, "All That You Love Will Be Carried Away" (as cited in Meyer, 2002)

From the point of view of an English teacher, one thing that jumps off the page for me is the use of the standard rhetorical patterns we all learned in the first term of college composition— description (details and examples), definition, comparison-contrast, classification, causal analysis. Each writer, of course, has a distinctive writing style. Both Poe and King use descriptive details to paint a scene and create mood, while Dickens uses comparison and contrast to introduce the concept of dual cities in a time of societal extremes. All three, however leave the reader intrigued and wanting to know more about the characters and what fate has in store for them. They have laid a solid foundation for their fictional houses.

Sentence Structure

Without getting too technical in terms of English grammar, let me move on the true building block of any piece of writing—the sentence. In English, the basic pattern of a simple sentence is SVO, or subject-verb-object.

S   V   O

The batter hit the ball.

Figure 12.2: Subjevct-Verb-Object

When children first learn to write in complete sentences, it looks something like this:

> My mom is nice. She makes my lunch and dinner. She tucks me in at night. Then she gives me a goodnight kiss. I love my mom.

Notice the familiar pattern of subject-verb-object in every sentence. This may be endearing in a child just learning to write, but does little to engage the reader. In order to break this monotonous, choppy-sounding pattern, the writer needs to vary the structure and length of sentences. Try not to make a habit of revising short, choppy sentences by simply stringing together main clauses using *and, or,* or *but.*

Example: She ate dinner. She washed her plate. She dried it and put it away.

Revision: She ate her dinner, and then she washed her plate, and then dried it and put it away.

Likewise, starting too many sentences with the same word, such as *The*, It, *This*, or *S/he,* can quickly become tedious for the reader. Changing sentence beginnings not only adds interest but may also alter both the structure and the emphasis of the sentence. Listed below are some common methods for varying sentence beginnings.

(1) Begin with an adverb or adverbial clause.

Methodically, she ate dinner, washed and dried her plate, and put it away.
(adverb describes *how*)

As soon as she finished eating dinner, she washed her plate, dried it, and put it away.
(adverbial clause)

(2) Begin with a prepositional or verbal phrase.

After dinner, she washed her plate, dried it, and put it away.
(prepositional phrase)

Finished with dinner, she washed her plate, dried it, and put it away.
(verbal phrase)

(3) Begin with a connecting word—a coordinating conjunction, conjunctive adverb, or transitional phrase.

> But tonight, she ate dinner, washed her plate, dried it, and put it away.
> (coordinating conjunction)
>
> Therefore, she ate dinner, washed her plate, dried it, and put it away.
> (conjunctive adverb)
>
> Even so, she ate dinner, washed her plate, dried it, and put it away.
> (transitional phrase)

(4) Begin with an appositive, an absolute phrase, or introductory series.

> A meticulous housekeeper, she washed her plate, dried it, and put it away.
> (appositive)
>
> Her appetite satisfied, she washed her plate, dried it, and put it away.
> (absolute phrase)
>
> Washing her plate, drying it, and putting it away—this was her typical after-dinner ritual.
> (introductory series)

In addition, breaking the pattern of subject-verb-object can be accomplished using these methods as well:

(5) Separate the subject and verb.

> She, always the meticulous housekeeper, washed her plate, dried it, and put it away.

(6) Add variety by using a question, an exclamation, or a command.

> How could she be expected to do otherwise than to follow her usual after-dinner ritual of washing her plate, drying it, and putting it away?
>
> Leave her plate on the table without washing it and putting it away? Never!

(Glenn, Miller, Webb, & Gray, 2004)

Word Choice

Show, Don't Tell

Effective writing tends to paint an image in the reader's mind instead of simply telling the reader what to think or believe. Think back to the opening paragraph of Poe's "Fall of the House of Usher." Not only did he use specific details that created a visual image, but he also appealed to the reader's other senses as well. One problem shared by many novice writers is the failure to provide specific detail. The solution, summed up in an old adage well-known among writers, is "show, don't tell."

Here is a sentence that tells: *Mr. Bowers was a fat, cranky old man.* Although there is some basic information provided about Mr. Bowers, the sentence is telling the reader what to think about him. By way of contrast, here is an example of writing which creates an image of Mr. Bowers in the reader's mind:

> Mr. Bowers heaved himself out of the chair. As his feet spread under his apple-shaped frame and his arthritic knees popped and cracked in objection, he pounded the floor with his cane while cursing that dreadful girl who was late again with his coffee.

In the second example, the writer did not say that Mr. Bowers is fat. Instead, she showed it by describing how he rose from the chair and comparing his frame to an apple. Neither did she say he was old, but implied that he was advanced in age by describing his arthritic knees and mentioning that he uses a cane. Nowhere in the second example do you see the word *cranky* either, but the combined actions of pounding his cane on the floor and cursing his caregiver cause the reader to conclude that Mr. Bowers is cranky. Also notable about the second example is the use of sensory details that appeal to both sight and to hearing, drawing the reader into the scene (Fogarty, 2015).

Synonyms

Nothing annoys me more as a reader than to encounter exactly the same word used multiple times on a single page. This problem seems to be closely related to the "show, don't tell" principle in that the writer should not have to continually remind the reader that someone is depressed or nervous or excited as long as the character's actions reflect that mental or emotional state. However, if a descriptive word is needed, a quick check of the online Thesaurus reveals a list of 47 synonyms for the word *depressed*. Among the more formal entries are *despondent, morose, dejected, disconsolate, crestfallen,* and *melancholy* while more informal expressions include *bummed out, down and out, down in the dumps, in the pits, torn up,* and *crummy.* (Synonyms for Depressed, n.d.)

Effective writers also add impact to their prose through the use of *vivid verbs,* descriptive action words that are so vibrant and dramatic that they help the reader visualize the word. Generally speaking, these verbs may describe sounds (*crackle, guffaw*), smells (*reek, permeate*), and movements (*plunge, swoop.*) For example, consider the common action verb *walk.* Now visualize the different ways to *walk* when one of these synonyms is substituted instead: *amble, lurch, pace, plod, prance, saunter, shuffle, skip, stagger, stride, traipse.* (Examples of Vivid Verbs, n.d.)

One of the most common pitfalls for writers related to synonyms seems to occur when writing dialogue. There are certainly times when it makes sense to use the word *said;* other times, the sense of the conversation being reported may be better served with a synonym. Here, by category, is a condensed list of words that might be used to balance said in the voice tags of dialogue:

Synonyms for *said*—reporting:
> Added, advised, complained, continued, stated, announced, asserted, commented, declared, informed, observed, offered, protested, quoted, remarked, repeated, replied, revealed, teased

Synonyms for *said*— explaining:
> Addressed, answered, asserted, cautioned, claimed, concluded, described, implied, quipped, noted, promised, rejoined, responded, speculated, surmised

Synonyms for *said*—arguing:
> Accused, agreed, argued, commanded, contended, convinced, countered, chided, disagreed, emphasized,

exclaimed, interjected, maintained, objected, pleaded, proclaimed, proposed, reasoned, threatened, warned

Synonyms for *said*—suggesting:
Coaxed, hinted, implied, insinuated, intimated, pondered, suggested, urged

Synonyms for *said*—questioning:
Asked, begged, demanded, guessed, hypothesized, implored, inquired, insisted, pleaded, questioned, requested, wondered

Synonyms for *said*— acknowledging:
Acknowledged, admitted, affirmed, alleged, approved, avowed, conceded, confessed, denied, disclosed, divulged, jested, marveled, nodded, praised, revealed, uttered, volunteered

Synonyms for *said*— tone:
Barked, bawled, beamed, bellowed, bleated, boomed, cackled, chattered, cheered, choked, clucked, cried, croaked, crowed, declaimed, drawled, groaned, grumbled, grunted, jeered, joked, laughed, mimicked, mumbled, muttered, nagged, ordered, ranted, roared, scolded, shrieked, smirked, snapped, snarled, sneered, whispered

(Synonyms for Said, 2012)

This list is by no means exhaustive, but it does illustrate how many choices there are for a writer to balance word choices in dialogue.

Here is a sample dialogue from a story I wrote recently, with all the voice tags changed to *said:*

> Only when Martha could feel her daughter's warm breath on her hand did she dare to speak. "Good day to you, sir," she <u>said</u>. "Me and my daughter was just headed to our

neighbor's farm to deliver this pie," she <u>said</u>. "We didn't mean no harm." The man's dark eyes continued to glare at them behind the raised shotgun as she spoke.

"Which farm would that be?" he <u>said</u> in a demanding tone, still staring at her down the barrel of his 12-gauge.

"Why...the Campbell's, just over the ridge there." She pointed with her right index finger, her left hand still holding onto the pie. "Edna, the wife, she just had a baby, a son, and we was going to see how they was both doing," she <u>said</u>, struggling to sound calm.

Very deliberately, in what seemed to Martha like slow motion, the man lowered the shotgun until it pointed at the earth. "Well now, I reckon you must be telling the truth seeing as how I knowed that James's wife was with child. Ain't seen neither of them in a month of Sundays, though," he <u>said</u>, as he removed his hat and raked his fingers through his coal-black hair. Hat in hand, he ducked his head and <u>said</u>, somewhat remorsefully, "Name's Ivan, Ivan McKinnon."

"Martha," she <u>said</u>, "Martha Vaughn. And this here is Lily, my lily-of-the- valley." With that, Lily leaned sideways from behind her mother's skirts to reveal her whole curly head, not just her eyes. She openly stared at Ivan McKinnon but offered no word of greeting.

In context, which synonyms of *said* would you employ to best convey meaning in this dialogue?

Our fictional house is now complete, built by our own hands from the ground up. I hope this writing workshop has provided you with some tools you can use to improve your next attempt at writing fiction.

References

Dickens, C. (1859) *Tale of two cities.* Retrieved June 29, 2016, from http://literature.org/authors/dickens-charles/two-cities/

Examples of vivid verbs. (n.d.).Retrieved September 29, 2016, from www.reference.com

Fogarty, M. (2010). Show, don't tell [Web log post]. Retrieved June 29, 2016, from http://www.quickanddirtytips.com/grammar-girl/show-dont-tell

Glenn, C., Miller, R., Webb, S., & Gray, L. (2004) *Hodges' harbrace handbook* (15th ed.) Boston: Thomson Wadsworth.

Meyer, M. (Ed.). (2002). All that you love will be carried away. *The Bedford Introduction to Literature.* (81-89). Boston: Bedford/St. Martin's.

Poe, E. A. (1839). Fall of the House of Usher. Retrieved June 29, 2016, from http://www.eapoe.org/works/tales/usherf.htm

Synonyms for depressed. (n.d.). Retrieved June 30, 2016, from http://www.thesaurus.com/browse/depression

Synonyms for Said. (n.d.). Retrieved June 29, 2016, from http://www.synonyms-antonyms.com/synonyms-for-said.html

Time to Tell: Writing Memoir
Deborah Wilbrink

> "I knocked on doors and convinced people that they needed electricity."
>
> "Mom and Dad took me to the welfare office and left me there."
>
> "Would I continue a career in the Navy, or jump ship into the corporate engineering world?"
>
> "Cows have personality, and Wild Sue was super shy."
>
> "'There's nothing in my job description that says I have to type your letters.'"
>
> "My husband brought the 14-year-old orphan girl into our home; when I left, he divorced me for abandonment and married her, keeping our children."

The above quotes are from memoirs by everyday people. These people are not rock stars, actors, politicians; they are electricians, housewives, social workers, managers. Everyday people can write a memoir. Let us look at why you should, and how you can get started.

Why Memoir Matters
My story's just not that interesting.
Not so fast. Every story will become another important chapter in the fascinating genre of memoir, including yours. Memoir is a life story, told by the person who lived it, that focuses on important, key events. These events can be important to the individual, but often hold meaning and life lessons for others. For example, one story may be that of childbirth, and the emotions and lifestyle changes of becoming a mother. Set that story within the context of 1914 on the farm, in 1950 at an urban hospital, or in 1977

during the homebirth movement, or in 2016 at a birthing center. Each of these options results in different stories that each shed light on a dark spot in history. Each of these stories belongs in someone's memoir. A family history may contain them all!

A memoir can be very personal, or it can be collection of family stories. Often, people want to record memories of older family members or assist another family member in writing their stories. All of these works fall into a broader genre called personal history. A journey alone through the wilderness is a type of memoir; the story of growing up on a dairy in North Carolina that includes stories about aunts and grandparents is a memoir. But, if that same author writes about the life in a town using stories from his aunts and grandparents, the work becomes a family history. The family history preserves not only your point of view, but also events and wisdom from days long gone by. Genealogy is the record of one's lineage and ancestry, often supplemented by stories. One can add genealogy to the family history, or just keep the stories. Which kind of memoir are you considering?

If you have thought about saving your individual life story so that others can read or view it, you are not alone. Memoir writing is an increasingly popular activity, and books of memoir are scattered throughout the best seller lists. After all, "truth is stranger than fiction," and true stories have the advantage of grabbing us right in the heart. If it happened to this person, it could happen to us! Other times, the enticement of a true story is that we have not and never will live in that manner. A memoir can be a jet to another time and place, a train across the continent of experience, or a subway roaring through another's subconscious and rising to shared revelation.

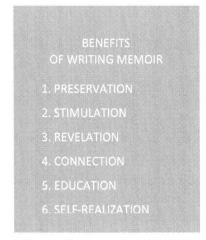

BENEFITS
OF WRITING MEMOIR

1. PRESERVATION

2. STIMULATION

3. REVELATION

4. CONNECTION

5. EDUCATION

6. SELF-REALIZATION

Figure 13.1
Benefits of Writing Memoir

Whether you are writing your memoir or a family history, the process itself offers six excellent benefits. With each advantage, I have coupled a tried and true technique to help you fully experience that benefit. In the process of reaping the benefit and using the technique, you will be writing your personal history!

Preservation

Some say that the spirit endures three deaths in this world: when the body dies, when the body is buried, and when it is finally forgotten. You can ensure that these spirit's stories— with their wisdom, pathos, and humor; their first-hand experience of a world unique and passing— will endure. Many people experience sorrow at the thought of what they have not saved: the stories of loved ones long gone. People still carry the fragments of those stories, and their children may be shaking their heads one day unless someone records the memories now.

In the event you find your home or that of another cluttered with keepsakes that have sentimental value, here is a way to clean out your sentimental closet. Photograph the objects that you love and pair those photos with text: a description of *who, where,* and *when.* Why is the item important enough to be kept? Whether using a photograph and a notebook page, or a digital photo and a word processing file, keep these together. Each object can be developed into a story. Think of this memoir finished, with a title. It could be called *Identified Objects.* Cleaning out the sentimental closet can also assist with cleaning out a real area. Once the memories and emotional value are preserved, parting with the objects themselves is easier. This technique can ease the pain of downsizing or moving, as well as generate memories for your memoir.

Stimulation

Writing a memoir stimulates many different mental processes. You may find that you enjoy corresponding, looking at old photos, and simply telling that special story as you compose your memoir. Recalling, writing, organizing, and planning use different parts of the brain. Learning new skills, meeting new people that help with your project, and practicing formal thought are all enjoyable mental exercises. When you are ready to take your writing into book form, you will develop even more skills and contacts. You will be considering how to use photographs as illustrations or whether to use only text for your memoir. Your motivation to preserve and share your memories and life lessons becomes a powerhouse that can energize learning new skills and perseverance.

You will need that perseverance, for there are several stages to writing before book completion. However, if you view your memoir as a personal project, then you will enjoy it immensely, thus lightening the pressure lightens considerably. One way to keep fun as a major part of the project is to *Use Your Natural Creativity*. What do you really enjoy doing (besides writing)? Make that hobby or passion a part of your memoir. Remember, every life is different. Your book needs to reflect *your* interests and life's themes. I love quilts, so when I wrote *Time to Tell: Your Personal & Family History,* I used graphic elements from quilts to illustrate the lessons and stories about personal history. The table below shows how four different passions could result in different books about the same life story.

Table 13.1
Integrating Passions

PASSION	INTEGRATION INTO MEMOIR	TITLES
Collecting Buttons	Openings and closings of life's chapters; events that the buttons remind one of experiencing; intermittent delights that collecting brought	*Keeping It Together* *Button Up!*
Gardening	Use gardening obstacles and solutions as metaphors for life challenges; divide your life story into the four seasons; tell the story of different gardens within the context of life events.	*The Seasons of My Life*
A Football Team	Parallel the timeline with that of the team's; use team colors throughout the book; compare event to something that happened to a player.	*Go, You Ugly Dawg!* *In the Shadow of the Titans* *Tiger Prowling! / A Tiger Burns Bright!*
Scrapbooking	Include fascination for preservation and sharing; illustrate chapter openings like an elaborate scrapbook page; mix topics in a loose organizational structure.	*Marty's Bits and Pieces* *Building from Scrap* *Saving Those Scraps*

Some writers will read these ideas and have an epiphany while others may sneer. That is fine; you should make your book in your own way and with joy.

Revelation

A memoir is a chance to tell the truth as you see it. While history is written and rewritten, you can tell others what actually happened— personally and historically— in memoir. You were there. While digging for these memories, you will be surprised at the incidents; as you research, some gaps will be filled that give a whole new meaning to the past.

Memory skills are an important talent for a memoir writer. Making an outline of events can tickle dormant memories awake. Some writers start with a list or timeline of key events and write these individual events as they feel inspiration or to meet set goals: write one event a day, one a week, etc. Others are more comfortable writing when they remember something and then organizing later. Memory is fleeting, so be sure to jot down a quick, typically one-line note when inspiration visits you—e.g. "Calvin's hat becomes a UFO"; if you are otherwise busy, you can return to that note later to write that story.

Several techniques can help transfer your memories from the forgotten status to active material for a memoir and its revelations. One is to work with *Show and Tell for Adults*. Martie McNabb, a personal historian in New York City, pioneered this enjoyable event for the Association of Personal Historians to adopt. Often during May, Personal History Awareness Month, people have an opportunity to meet for a show and tell. If an event is not available in your area, then you can organize one. McNabb renamed her events *Show and Tales*, and they take place in bars as often as not.

You can use this concept to generate some great stories or to help you record memories. Use it at a party, a family reunion, a dinner, or simply on a visit to learn more about family history by asking guests to bring an object or photo from the past. Some will bring a document, a letter, or an award. Participants take turns sharing stories about the item they brought. These stories make enjoyable conversation pieces and ice-breakers and are a way to hear new family stories. I have led many Show and Tell events at retirement communities, senior centers, and churches. I learned so much from so many about the past at these events. One man showed a homemade toy and told us, "When I was a child, the goat man would lead our annual parade. One year, my grandpa gave me a toy goat cart. I still have it." The man slowly placed his treasure upon the table for us all to see. He smilingly viewed the toy, remembering both the goat man and his grandfather. We could still see the boy who enjoyed and wondered at the world in his precious smile.

While parades of goats and transportation by goat cart have faded from our world, they were quite common at one time. One goat man, Ches McCartney, is particularly famous. Details like these can enhance the story if you take some time to research your objects. Some folks are so thrilled with the significance of their personal treasure that they forget to explain it to others. How did it arrive? What made it significant? Why is it still kept and treasured? With a little thoughtful digging, the object can bring back memories that seemed lost forever. Writers can use yesterday's treasures to explain differences in the past for younger readers. This practice makes the story a real journey into the past. As a writer, you will do more than show, tell, and smile with your object.

You can see and hold the object, even if just in your mind's eye. When you write, you must help others imagine the object and its story. What does it look like, feel like, sound like, smell like, or taste like? What are you seeing, hearing, touching, feeling, smelling, tasting when you go hand in hand with that object down Memory Lane?

Just as you want others to appreciate your stories, you should be sure to thank anyone who shares a memory with you.

Education

Storytelling is the oldest form of education. If you learned something the hard way, or have a valuable skill, please share that in your memoir.

Many people have unique experiences and skills. Ninety-eight-year old Thaddeus Martin was proud of being the last living person in his union, Maritime Electrical Engineers. He had joined during World War II and wired the great ships that transported and fought the war. He wanted to tell that and much more, creating more conversation with his great-grandchildren. With his memoir in its final stages, Thad had a restless night. He called me the next day, saying, "We have to have a story in there about how to butcher a pig. No one knows how to do that anymore!" Certainly not the way it was done in 1926 on Thad's mother's farm.

One year after publication, Thad's family was listening to their minister read the stories about Thad Martin's religious experiences from *That's the Gist of It* (2012) at his Celebration of Life. Their elder had passed, but everyone was still laughing at his stories. His spirit was there, and his great-grandchildren saw love and respect for him all around them. Because Thad wrote his memoir, he will remain a legend in his family.

Mary Mallen was determined to make something of her journals and notes. She wrote a memoir for her daughters' families titled *Stops Along the Way* (2014). The theme of this memoir is that "optimism and enthusiasm will get you through the hardships." She recollects her participation in the changes of the travel industry. Mary started life in a traveling house trailer but ended up revolutionizing airline sales. To read her memoir is to forever appreciate the ease, cost, and speed of today's travel, and how it came to be.

Yes, memoir is an entertaining educational tool. The story could be one to trigger universal learning, as in writing about the topic "my first job, and what I learned there about work." Many books and websites offer memoir writing prompts. Use such a prompt to inspire and to educate, working alone or with a writers group, where all will learn.

Self-Realization

Recollecting and recording, you will find yourself revisiting choices that you made or had made for you. You have a whole life of wisdom to aid in this reflection. You may find that you see the past in a different light this time around. Memoir can be therapeutic and an aid to spiritual development.

In writing one story, "The Experiment," for my memoir, I recall how I bucked the established rules as a young person, wanting to find out everything firsthand. In every case, I undertook an adventure that, unfortunately, proved the rule. These adventures made for an exciting story, and I hope they will convey some wisdom. For every time I read a memoir, I learn a lesson. Often, the entire memoir will develop a moral theme, whether work ethic, familial love, a cheerful attitude that overcomes adversity, or something else.

A list of "Advice I've always wanted to give my kids" makes for an interesting group session and will result in stories based on experience; stories that educate and often lead to realization. List advice you would like to give others. Now, how did you learn that? Write the story behind the advice, and you have an important story for your memoir— one that educates as well as entertains.

You, too, have life lessons to teach. Your voice of experience speaks with authority. Your real legacy is your wisdom. Now is the time to prepare those lessons for future readers. You have a unique perspective. Teach others and help them avoid mistakes. Rough times and even bad choices were often good teachers. These amazing true lessons of life show our human side and create reader interest. What can you teach?

Instead of moralizing, let the reader deduce the lesson from a story that included your motivation, actions, and consequences. A successful exception to "show don't tell" is often found in older texts and can be used by modern writers. A quote, an epigram, a proverb, or a scriptural verse can deliver your lesson succinctly, either at the beginning or end of a chapter. The writer of the Biblical book of Ecclesiastes offers us some memoir-writing advice:

"There is a time for everything, and a season for every activity under the heavens...a time to search and a time to give up, a time to keep and a time to throw away, a time to tear and a time to mend, a time to be silent and a time to speak..." (Eccles. 3:1, 6-7, NIV)

Connection

Writing a memoir can provide stronger connections to family, create new friendships, and connect you to a wider world of similar interests.

Memoirs that include stories from your youth or about your family can bring you closer to relatives in unexpected ways. Email has opened paths to faster communication, and the messages do not always have to be terse. Margaret Wells Hayslip began emailing excerpted tidbits from her grandmother's journals to family members in anticipation of a family reunion. Later, she developed her family history book, *If You Care to Keep the Last Letter,* around her grandmother's journals and collection of family memorabilia, and she sold welcomed copies at the next family reunion. Margaret's father provided encouragement with the large project, and cousins chipped in with photographs. A memoir can also be a beauteous, treasured heritage gift that will keep a person's memory alive for generations to come.

For Marion Mingle in Nashville, USA, and her sister Anne Strang in Sydney, Australia, writing their book *Growing Up in Glasgow: A Conversation Between Sisters* (2016) uncovered a mystery. The sisters grew up in Glasgow, Scotland, but shared few memories. They knew little about their father. After Anne asked what Marion remembered, there ensued a two-week email binge across continents and time zones, with different stories emerging for fact-checking and review. For a private memoir, the sisters collected their emails, paired them with photos for illustrations, and published a heritage book for the two families. As a by-product, the sisters are engaging in more conversation with friends and senior group members, connecting.

More conventionally, many families travel to obtain stories and collaborate. This is a skill you will need for all memoirs. Consider collaboration with someone whose skills and time available can complement your own. It may be a relative who is also interested. There may be a "kin-keeper" in your family, the go-to person who saves the stories, the photographs, and whatever you may have of genealogy and family trees. Another person may be willing to spend time recording and editing your story. It may be a paid ghostwriter or personal historian. It may be simply sharing and critiquing with a writing group. Find people with like interests and helpful skills, and you have found fun and society. Your project will need the talents of research, storytelling, writing, and editing as well as an eye for design and some computer skills, like those of scanning photos or exploring genealogy online. Finally, and most importantly, practice patience and determination. Then, it is off to your local book printer or preferred print-on-demand (POD) online publishing site— though, this may be the collaborator's job.

Publication of your memoir for general readers opens another world that could bring you into collaboration with agents, publishers, public relations agencies, book stores, and book festivals. You will need help even if your book is a potential bestseller. If your memoir is for friends and family, then its publication can be an event, too. Throw a party!

There is always a danger of losing your connections by writing honestly. Write the truth; however, consult a lawyer if you are painting a dark picture of another person, especially one who is living. Some memoir writers tell painful stories with the thought of editing those parts out later, but those stories are actually seldom omitted. Pain and challenges connect with readers and can help them on the path of life.

Every path is traveled one step at a time. Take one step at a time writing your memoir, and start with the part you enjoy most. You will learn new skills and make new, helpful friends along the way. Do not be disheartened or daunted. The backstory of personal history is the story of people growing as they face the challenges and meet the helpmates of their project.

Avoiding Common Mistakes

In my own journey as an editor-for-hire, ghostwriter, and author, I have benefited from reading many manuscripts. It is a pleasure to work with many first-time authors who turn out to be radiant, beautiful people with fascinating stories to tell. In the process of seeing these manuscripts, I have come to note some needed general advice for memoir writers:

Write about the memorable, not just memories.

Losing car keys and waiting for help is a familiar experience. Readers do not want to read a play-by-play account of it. Unless, that is, you met your spouse that way; it was an old car on a dirt road, and you waited three days for the right part to come; or your job depended on that nigh-impossible delivery.

Keep yourself likeable most of the time.

No matter how you may have been victimized or hurt, no one enjoys reading a brew of bitterness. Tell the same facts, but try different approaches: two sides to the story, environmental background, anger and what was done about it, or a lesson learned.

Hold your questions till last.

Sometimes, interrupting a train of thought can completely derail the train. When conducting interviews or listening to a storytelling session, make a note of any details you want to ask about before writing these true stories but do not stop the speaker in the midst. Even if the story wanders, it may go to another interesting place. The same applies when you are writing your own story. Put your internal editor down for a nap during your first draft and hold your factual research for later.

Include feelings and emotions.

"We were playing croquet when Dad fell down and died. We called the undertaker. The funeral was three days later." These sentences convey a numbness, but is it intentional style? Or does the writer need to work on conveying his feelings? Be sure that a lack of appropriate emotion is a choice, not an oversight. What do you want to communicate to your readers?

Write conversations into your memoir.

A story becomes more real when voiced. The memoir's cast need words. You may not remember a woman's exact words, but you will remember her tone, how she spoke, some pet sayings. How did this person stand when they delivered a lecture or were excited, happy, sad? Some writers choose to write completely in dialog; others use one or two sentences here and there for emphasis during the story. Dialog helps make a story come alive for the reader, even if the quote is how it could have been said rather than verbatim.

End your story and share it.

Genealogists and researchers know that any book based on facts can be researched endlessly. When a writer has a good story with a reasonable amount of research, it is time to tell. Those notebooks in the closet may end up thrown out rather than treasured, but a finished book will stay on the table, on the shelf, and in the county archives. Maybe even on the World Wide Web. Many people stop writing mid-tale because they don't know what to say next. Seek out other writers for advice and recommendations.

Use an editor or, at least, a proof reader.
By now, you have probably seen an error, or more, in this copter. We see more errors in published works today – Like the computer EMERAC in the movie *Desk Set* (1957), our use of spell check is good at some things but not so good at others. I have also seen some horrendous self-published books that are barely readable. While asking a friend to check your work is better than asking no one— and a friend who is an English teacher is even better— you can also find reasonably-priced professionals. If you are spending hours, maybe years, on your memoir, does it not deserve to be presented in its best suit, not the one in tatters and rags? A proofreader checks for spelling and mechanical errors— i.e. the rules of grammar and punctuation. An editor will give advice about what needs clarification and what is superfluous.

Keep your personal voice.
Do not let an editor or your own insecurity clean up your written language to the point that you sound like someone else. Colloquialisms and dialect? *Good to go!* Personal idioms? Don't get *red as a beet* over that! *All is in the middle*! Older generations sometimes use different sentence structures and longer sentences. A memoir should let them retain their voice, the voice of an older, more eloquent, slower-paced way of life.

Be happy with the journey.
The benefits of memoir are seldom financial ones. Believing that your book will go viral or that everyone will want to read your unique story is easy, but the hard truth is that most authors will spend many hours, or pay a highly-skilled person, to achieve sales for their first book. Before writing a memoir, you must decide if

you will be happy with any result or if you have a specific goal for the book. Many memoir authors are happy in the process and find joy in leaving a legacy for their family without the added effort of marketing. What will make you happiest in writing your memoir?

The "Time to Tell" is now! Many people have an idea for a memoir that stays with them for years. It is important to act on that idea. Writing or recording your life story comes easily to some and seems difficult to others. Make time for this important project, and you will find lots of enjoyment as you proceed. So put away your fears and procrastination, and take up your pen or recorder.

Additional Resources

Association of Personal Historians, the professional international trade association with information and resources: www.PersonalHistorians.org

Perfect Memoirs, website of personal historian, writer and memoir educator, Deborah Wilbrink: www.perfectmemoirs.com

Time to Tell: Your Personal & Family History by Deborah Wilbrink is a how-to book with examples in story, song and poems for the do-it-yourself family historian or memoir writer. Available from Amazon.com or from your local bookstore.

Author Bios

Carissa (Cat) Barker-Stucky, M.F.A.

Cat works as a freelance writer, editor, and graphic designer. She has been with Carnegie Writers, Inc. since February 2015 and is currently the Chair of the Publications Committee.

Carissa graduated from Southwest Baptist University with a Bachelor of Art in English in December 2011, graduated from Lindenwood University with a Master of Fine Arts in Writing in December 2012 and married Christopher at the stroke of midnight January 1st, 2013. She now lives in Arkansas with the love of her life and their multitude of pets—as of this publication, they have a Labrador/Beagle mutt mix (Lucy), a Great Pyrenese/Blue heeler mix (Astro), a Domestic Short-Hair cat (Kevin-Kupo), a Domestic Medium-Hair cat (Hoot), two Mini Rex rabbits (Susuwatari and CinnaBunBun), and a Bearded Dragon (Felix). She dreams o becoming a published Fantasy author, but untll then she has plenty to keep her busy. Nothing inspires her more than a cup of Chai Tea Latte and a purring kitten on her lap.

Kristen Billingsley

Kristen was born in 1991 in Alabama, where she grew up and went to college. Kristen discovered her love for writing when she was 12 and attempted to write a vampire romance when she was 15. At the age of 21, she published *Gemini of Emréiana* before writing and publishing its sequel, *Gemini the Heir.* She is currently working on the last book of the series, *Gemini a Legacy* and other titles.

When she is not writing, Kristen is an avid reader and TV junkie. She has a not-so-secret love for K-dramas and anime. In her spare time, she likes to play video games—anything from Sims to *Battlefront.*

Kristen currently lives in Nashville with her number one supporter— her husband, musician Patrick Ryan. They live with their two dogs (Amai and Henri) and are expecting their first son, Elliott, in late summer.

Oluwakemi (Kemi) Elufiede, M.Ed

Kemi holds 10 years of professional experience in public, community (education), non-profit sector, and social services. She is the Founder and President of Carnegie Writers, Inc. and K&E Educational Consulting Services, where she provides assistance in writing, editing, non-profit management, and life coaching. Prior to entrepreneurship, Elufiede assumed many roles as a tutor, teacher, mentor, instructor, evaluations manager, case manager, and residence director. She has presented at over 20 professional conferences and workshops and has facilitated over 30 programs in areas such as residence life, leadership development, writing, literacy, technology, career and workforce development, effective tutoring strategies, mental health, self-directed learning, community education, adult learning, and mentoring.

Kemi holds a degree in P-12 Special Education from Abraham Baldwin Agricultural College, B.L.S in Psychology and M.Ed in Adult Education and Community Leadership from Armstrong Atlantic State University. She is Doctoral Candidate in Educational Leadership with a concentration in higher education at Tennessee State University. She is the editor and author of five books and has several academic publications.

Bonnie Flynn, Ed.D., MPH., MS

Dr. Bonnie Flynn is an Associate Professor of Health Studies in the College of Professional Studies and Advancement (CPSA) at National Louis University (NLU). She holds a Doctorate in Adult and Continuing Education from NLU, a Master in Public Health from Benedictine University, and master degrees in both Adult Education and Written Communication from NLU. Dr. Flynn has designed and taught courses in blended and online formats. She is an active member of the American Association of Adult and Continuing Education (AAACE) and the Adult Higher Education Alliance (AHEA).

Tavia Garland, MPA

Tavia Garland graduated in 2012 with a Master's in Non-Profit Management and Leadership. She is currently working on a Ph.D., also in Non-Profit Management and Leadership. She has helped multiple non-profits expand their programs through grant writing and leadership guidance and founded her own non-profit animal rescue in 2009, based in Nashville. Currently employed by the American Red Cross, she works daily to assist those in need in the community as well as expanding her non-profit leadership experience. She currently serves on the Carnegie Writer's Board of Directors, sits on the Finance Committee, and functions as the primary Grant Writer for the organization. She is also working on expanding her freelance writing career in her spare time. She resides in Nashville, TN with her dogs, Llyric and Jazz, and also pursues interests in other arts, such as acting, dance, and painting.

Kay Gragg

Kay Gragg, a native Nashvillian, earned a B.A. degree in English from Lambuth University in Jackson, Tennessee, and an M.A. from the University of Tennessee, Knoxville. She retired from her teaching position with Metropolitan Nashville Public Schools in 2014, and over the course of her career in education has taught every level of English/Language Arts from seventh grade through college composition. Since retiring, Kay balances her love of gardening with her renewed passion for reading and writing.

Jamie Hughes

Jamie Hughes is the founder of Writing for Well-Being, which offers life-changing therapeutic writing courses. After graduating Gardner-Webb University with a degree in psychology, he went on to become a certified journal writing instructor. Jamie has spent the last decade educating others from a holistic, God-centered viewpoint about effective understanding and treatment of depression, especially through writing. A published author and editor, he also enjoys painting and mosaic artwork. He lives in the upstate of SC with his wife and children on the Happy Hens Farm where the chickens are named after superheroes.

LaDessa Mitchell

LaDessa Mitchell has an extensive history of work in nonprofit organizations as a volunteer and in various leadership capacities throughout the Tampa Bay Area. She has worked with various age groups, programs and populations throughout her tenure. She began mentoring in 2003 while attending college. Currently, Mrs. Mitchell is the Executive Director of the nonprofit MERGE Inc., an organization helping student pursue higher education. She earned a Bachelor of Science in Applied Economics and three minors (Business, Psychology, and Religion) from Florida State University ('06). She graduated from The University of Tampa ('10) with a Master of Business Administration and graduate certificate in Nonprofit Management. Mrs. Mitchell received scholarships from Miss Tallahassee USA 2004 pageant for her volunteer work and from the Institute of Management Accountants (IMA) in 2008 for her excellence in academics. She is doctoral student working towards a Ph.D. in Curriculum & Instruction at University of South Florida ('18). She a wife and mother of four children.

Tina Murray, Ph.D.

Tina Murray is the author of two novels, *A Chance to Say Yes* and *A Wild Dream of Love*, both published by ArcheBooks. In addition, she served as co-editor of the nonfiction anthology, *Enhancing Writing Skills*, published by Information Age Publishing. Currently, she holds the position of vice president of Carnegie Writers, Inc. Other activities include reading scripts for the Nashville Film Festival's screenwriting competition and pursuing an interest in songwriting. Her third novel, *A Big Fan of Yours*, will be available soon.
Website: http://www.tinamurrayauthor.com

Brian Smith

Brian Smith is a freelance writer. He graduated from Belmont University in 2016 with a BA in English. During his time at Belmont, he worked as an editor on the Belmont Literary Journal, helped facilitate a Carnegie Writers adult writing workshop, and tutored a First Year Writing class. He was also published in the Belmont Literary Journal and won first place in the Sandra Hutchins Poetry Contest. He lives in Nashville, TN.

Carol Roberts

Carol Roberts is a writer (and reader), a grandmother, a blogger and a woman who believes in the power of words to inspire and sometimes even to change a life. She has worked as a secretary, Christian minister, teacher and activities assistant. It was while working at a rehabilitation facility that she discovered the healing power of words. She has two blogs: lifestory.solutions and poetryforthejourney.com.

Annie Laura Smith

Annie Laura Smith has publications in the areas of fiction and nonfiction for children, curriculum materials for children and adults, general interest, inspirational and technical articles, book reviews, test materials, and poetry.

She was an instructor for the Institute of Children's Literature. In addition to her published World War II historical novels, historical romance novel, contemporary YA novel, and young reader biographies, she co-authored a First Grade Math Textbook for Ethiopia under a USAID grant, and adapted the classic, The Pioneers, by James Fenimore Cooper to Reading Level 4 for the EDCON Publishing Group.

She is available for classroom visits, presentations, conferences and writing courses.

Contact: annielaurasmith@comcast.net

Jaden Terrell

Jaden Terrell is a Shamus award finalist, the internationally published author of the *Jared McKean* private detective series, and a contributor to Now Write! Mysteries, a collection of exercises published by Tarcher/Penguin for writers of crime fiction. Her short stories have appeared in *Killer Nashville Noir: Coldblooded* and *Eight Mystery Writers You Should Be Reading Now*, and she writes a regular column for the *Killer Nashville Magazine*. The recipient of the 2009 Magnolia Award for service to the Southeastern Chapter of Mystery Writers of America, Terrell is also a writing coach, workshop leader, and developmental/content editor. Learn more at: http://www.jadenterrell.com.

T.K. Thorne

T.K. Thorne's childhood passion for storytelling deepened when she became a police officer in Birmingham, Alabama. Her writing has garnered several awards, including a ForeWord Reviews "Book of the Year" for her debut historical novel *Noah's Wife*, a Benjamin Franklin and IPPY award for her newest historical novel about the unnamed wife of Lot, *Angels at the Gate*. Her debut non-fiction, *Last Chance for Justice* gives the investigators' story of the 1963 Sixteenth Street church bombing case and was featured on the *New York Post*'s "Books You Should Be Reading" list. She loves traveling to research her novels and speaking about her books and life lessons and writes at her mountaintop home near Birmingham, often with two dogs and a cat vying for her lap. www.tkthorne.com

Deborah Wilbrink

Deborah Wilbrink, BJ, is author of *Time to Tell Your Personal & Family History*, and a personal historian who has helped others write and publish over twenty-five memoir and family history books through her business, Perfect Memoirs. She is Secretary of the Association of Personal Historians, columnist for Mature Lifestyles of Tennessee and regularly speaks to groups and teaches writing workshops. Deborah is a former English teacher, historic cemetery manager, and television news producer and editor. She lives with her husband in Nashville, Tennessee, where she sometimes enjoys gardening and performing her original songs. Her vice is carefully reading library books—while in the bath.

Contact: 615-417-8424
deb@PerfectMemoirs.com
www.PerfectMemoirs.com

Made in the USA
Lexington, KY
07 November 2016